Key Stage 2 Maths

Numerical Reasoning Technique

WORKBOOK **7**

Dr Stephen C Curran

with Katrina MacKay

Edited by Andrea Richardson

This book belongs to

Accelerated Education Publications Ltd

Contents

12. Percentages

		Pages
1.	What is a Percentage?	3-6
2.	Percentages & Fractions	7-8
3.	Percentages & Decimals	9-10
4.	Fractions, Decimals & Percentages	11-13
5.	Percentage Calculations	14-15
6.	Problem Solving	15-16

13. Probability

1.	What is Probability?	17-18
2.	Equal Probabilities	18-20
3.	Possible Outcomes	20-21
4.	Calculating Probability	22-23
5.	Problem Solving	24-25

14. Lines & Angles

1.	Types of Line	26-30
2.	Types of Angle	30-36
3.	Compass Directions	37-39

15. Time

1.	Time Measurement	40-45
2.	Dates	46-51
3.	The Analogue Clock	51-68
4.	12-hour Time	69-74
5.	24-hour Time	75-79
6.	12-hour & 24-hour Time	80-87
7.	Problem Solving	87-88

Chapter Twelve
PERCENTAGES
1. What is a Percentage?

A **Percentage** is a number out of **100**.

A percentage is shown by this symbol: **%**

One hundred per cent (100%) is the whole amount.

Percentages that are less than **100%** represent part of an amount. For example, **50%** is **half** of the total.

Percentages are often seen in shops, banks and advertisements.

Percentages can be shown on a grid of **100** squares.

1%
1 part of a hundred.

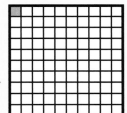

10%
10 parts of a hundred.

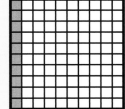

Example: What percentage of this grid is shaded?

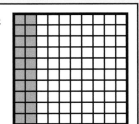

Count the number of shaded squares. There are **20** shaded squares out of a total of **100** squares. This means **20%** of the grid is shaded.

Answer: **20%**

Exercise 12: 1

Count the squares and write the % shaded:

1)

_____%

2)

_____%

3)

_____%

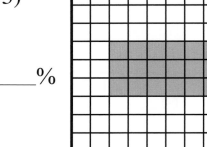

4)

_____%

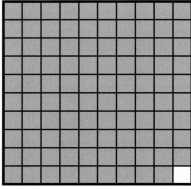

Shade in the percentage:

5)

62%

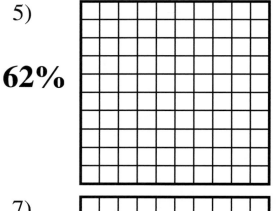

6)

35%

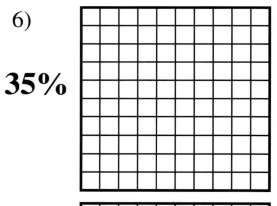

7)

77%

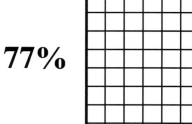

8)

43%

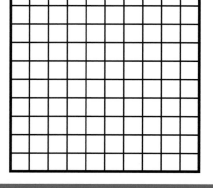

9) A smiley face has been shaded on a grid of **100** squares.

What percentage do the eyes and nose take up on the grid? _____%

10) Shade in a sad face in the same style on the grid below (the mouth flips upside-down):

What percentage of the grid does the whole face take up?

_____ %

Example: | If Robbie gives **60%** of his stamp collection to Malcolm, what percentage does he have left?

Robbie begins with **100%** of his stamp collection. He gives away **60%**. Subtract from **100%** to find what percentage Robbie has left of his stamp collection.

$$100\% - 60\% = 40\%$$

Answer: **40%**

Exercise 12: 2   Answer the following:

Score

1) If Shala gives **30%** of her trading cards to Laura, what percentage does she have left? _____

2) If Joelene gives **80%** of her pencils to Jenna, what percentage does she have left? _____

3) If Jason gives **65%** of his pens to Aroni, what percentage does he have left? _____

4) If Colin gives **15%** of his cakes to John, what percentage does he have left? _____

5) If Hira gives **40%** of her marbles to Gillian, what percentage does she have left? _____

6) If Seamus gives **90%** of his sweets to Emilia, what percentage does he have left? _____

7) If Hugh gives **20%** of his biscuits to Fay and **30%** to Hayley, what percentage does he have left? _____

8) If Andrea gives **10%** of her toys to Elliot and **20%** to Steven, what percentage does she have left? _____

9) If Jameen gives **35%** of her books to Michelle and **15%** to Mike, what percentage does she have left? _____

10) If Leia gives **25%** of her CDs to Kayleigh and **40%** to Daryl, what percentage does she have left? _____

6

2. Percentages & Fractions

Percentages can be written as **Fractions**, because they represent parts of a total or whole one. For example:

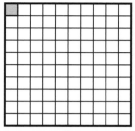

$$1\% = \frac{1}{100}$$

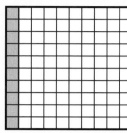

$$10\% = \frac{10}{100} = \frac{1}{10}$$

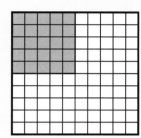

$$25\% = \frac{25}{100} = \frac{1}{4}$$

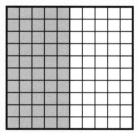

$$50\% = \frac{50}{100} = \frac{1}{2}$$

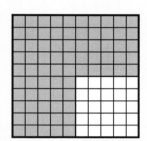

$$75\% = \frac{75}{100} = \frac{3}{4}$$

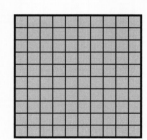

$$100\% = \frac{100}{100} = 1 \text{ whole}$$

Example:
Write the percentage of the first grid and its equal fraction for the second grid.

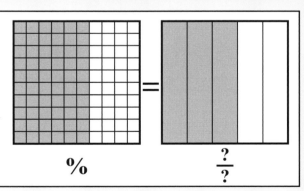

Step 1 - Count the number of shaded squares. There are **60** shaded squares out of a total of **100** squares, or $\frac{60}{100}$. This means **60%** of the first grid is shaded.

Step 2 - There are **3** shaded parts in the second grid, out of a total of **5** parts.
This means the equivalent fraction is $\frac{3}{5}$.

Answer: $\mathbf{60\%} = \frac{60}{100} = \frac{3}{5}$

Exercise 12: 3

Write the missing equivalent percentage or fraction:

1)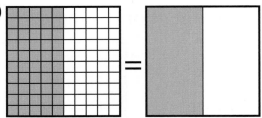

$$50\% \quad = \quad \underline{\hspace{2cm}}$$

2)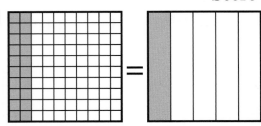

$$\underline{\hspace{2cm}} \quad = \quad \frac{1}{5}$$

3)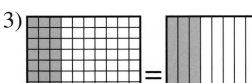

$$\underline{\hspace{2cm}} \quad = \quad \frac{3}{10}$$

4)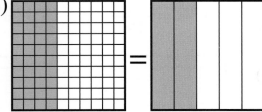

$$40\% \quad = \quad \underline{\hspace{2cm}}$$

5)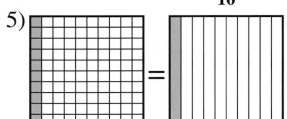

$$\underline{\hspace{2cm}} \quad = \quad \frac{1}{10}$$

6)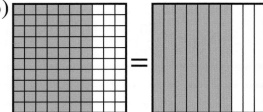

$$70\% \quad = \quad \underline{\hspace{2cm}}$$

7)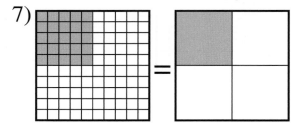

$$\underline{\hspace{2cm}} \quad = \quad \frac{1}{4}$$

8)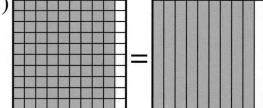

$$\underline{\hspace{2cm}} \quad = \quad \frac{9}{10}$$

9)

$$75\% \quad = \quad \underline{\hspace{2cm}}$$

10)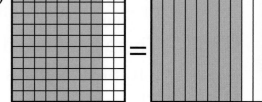

$$80\% \quad = \quad \underline{\hspace{2cm}}$$

3. Percentages & Decimals

Percentages can be written as **Decimals**, because they are parts of a whole. With percentages, a whole is **100%**. For example:

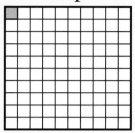

1% = 0.01
(One-hundredth)

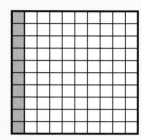

10% = 0.1
(One-tenth)

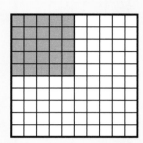

25% = 0.25
(One-quarter)

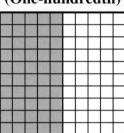

50% = 0.5
(One-half)

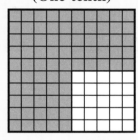

75% = 0.75
(Three-quarters)

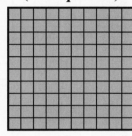

100% = 1.0
(One Whole)

Example: Write the percentage of the first grid and its equal decimal for the second grid.

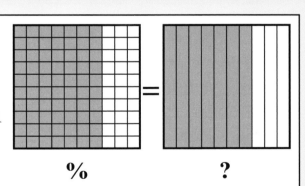

%   ?

Step 1 - Count the number of shaded squares. There are **70** shaded squares out of a total of **100** squares. This means **70%** of the first grid is shaded.

Step 2 - There are **7** shaded parts in the second grid, out of a total of **10** parts. This is **seven-tenths**. This means the equivalent decimal is **0.7**.

Answer: **70% = 0.7**

1)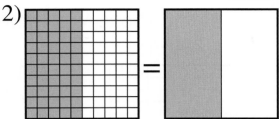

10% = _____

2)

_____ = **0.5**

3)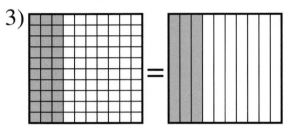

_____ = **0.3**

4)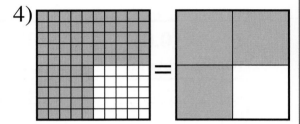

75% = _____

5)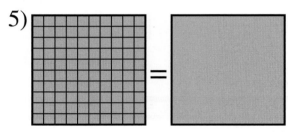

100% = _____

6)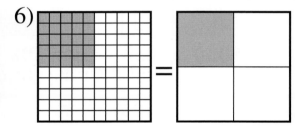

_____ = **0.25**

7)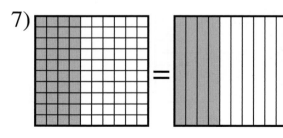

40% = _____

8)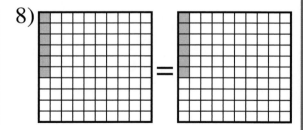

_____ = **0.06**

9)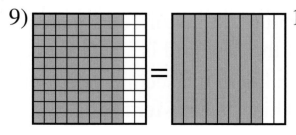

80% = _____

10)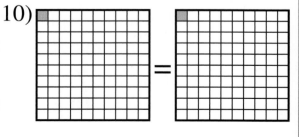

_____ = **0.01**

4. Fractions, Decimals & Percentages

Fractions, Decimals & Percentages are all ways of representing amounts. The same amount can be shown in three different ways.

The table shows useful equivalent conversions of fractions, decimals and percentages. It can be used to work out simple conversions.

For example, $\frac{9}{10} = 0.9 = 90\%$

Fraction	Decimal	Percentage
$\frac{1}{100}$	0.01	1%
$\frac{1}{10}$	0.1	10%
$\frac{1}{5}$	0.2	20%
$\frac{1}{4}$	0.25	25%
$\frac{1}{2}$	0.5	50%
$\frac{3}{4}$	0.75	75%

Example: Write the equivalent percentage, fraction and decimal for these grids.

Percentage   **Fraction**   **Decimal**

 = =

The three grids are all equal to each other.

Step 1 - Count the number of shaded squares. There are **40** shaded squares out of a total of **100** squares. This means **40%** of the first grid is shaded.

Step 2 - There are **2** shaded parts in the second grid, out of a total of **5** parts. The equivalent fraction is $\frac{2}{5}$.

Step 3 - There are **4** shaded parts in the third grid, out of a total of **10** parts, this is **four-tenths**. The equivalent decimal is **0.4**.

Answer: $\mathbf{80\%} = \frac{2}{5} = \mathbf{0.4}$

Exercise 12: 5

Write the equivalent percentage, fraction or decimal:

Percentage		Fraction		Decimal

1) 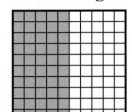 = 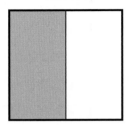 =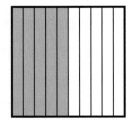

50% = _____ = **0.5**

2) 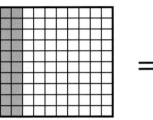 = =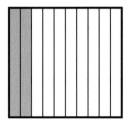

_____ = $\dfrac{1}{5}$ = **0.2**

3) 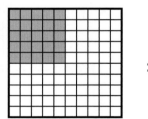 = 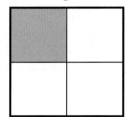 =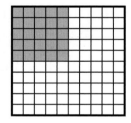

25% = $\dfrac{1}{4}$ = _____

4) 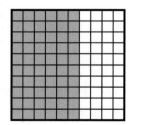 = =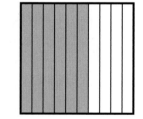

_____ = $\dfrac{3}{5}$ = **0.6**

5) 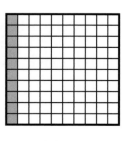 = 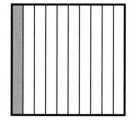 =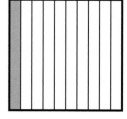

10% = _____ = **0.1**

Percentage		Fraction		Decimal

6) 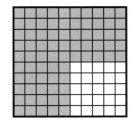 =  =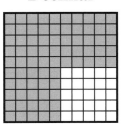

$$75\% \quad = \quad \frac{3}{4} \quad = \quad \underline{\qquad}$$

7) 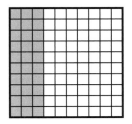 = 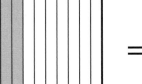 =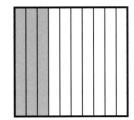

$$\underline{\quad}\% \quad = \quad \frac{3}{10} \quad = \quad \underline{\qquad}$$

8) 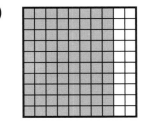 = 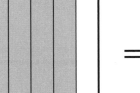 =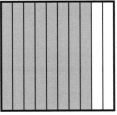

$$80\% \quad = \quad \underline{\qquad} \quad = \quad \underline{\qquad}$$

9) 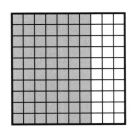 = 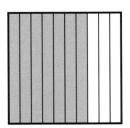 =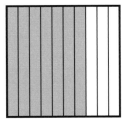

$$\underline{\qquad} \quad = \quad \underline{\qquad} \quad = \quad 0.7$$

10) 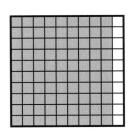 = 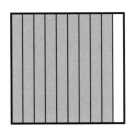 =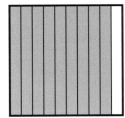

$$\underline{\quad}\% \quad = \quad \frac{9}{10} \quad = \quad \underline{\qquad}$$

5. Percentage Calculations
a. Simple % Calculations

Finding a percentage of a given amount can be easily done for certain percentages. Use the following to find:

1%	- or one-hundredth	- **divide by 100**
10%	- or one-tenth	- **divide by 10**
20%	- or one-fifth	- **divide by 5**
25%	- or one-quarter	- **divide by 4**
50%	- or one-half	- **divide by 2**

Example: Find **25%** of **80**.

To find **25%** is the same as finding **one-quarter**.

Divide by **4**   **80 ÷ 4 = 20**

Answer: **20**

Exercise 12: 6 Find the amount:

1) **50%** of **10p**. _____

2) **1%** of **600**. _____

3) **20%** of **100**. _____

4) **1%** of **800g**. _____

5) **50%** of **900**. _____

6) **25%** of **400**. _____

7) **10%** of **£70**. _____

8) **25%** of **20**. _____

9) **25%** of **80**. _____

10) **10%** of **500kg**. _____

b. Simple Two-step % Calculations

By dividing down or multiplying up, it is possible to do easy two-step calculations. For example to calculate:

4%   - find **1%** then multiply by **4**.

30% - find **10%** then multiply by **3**.

75% - find **25%** then multiply by **3**.

Example: | Find **40%** of **£60**. |

Step 1 - Find **10%** - divide by **10**

$$£60 ÷ 10 = £6$$

Step 2 - Find **40%** - multiply by **4**

$$£6 × 4 = £24$$

Answer: **£24**

Exercise 12: 7 Find the amount:

1) **90%** of **90**. _____

    10%: 90 ÷ 10 = __9__

    90%: __9__ × 9 = _____

2) **60%** of **600**. _____

    10%: 600 ÷ 10 = __60__

    60%: __60__ × 6 = _____

3) **75%** of **200**. _____

4) **9%** of **700**. _____

5) **70%** of **120**. _____

6) **5%** of **80p**. _____

7) **30%** of **£550**. _____

8) **40%** of **300kg**. _____

9) **80%** of **400**. _____

10) **2%** of **700g**. _____

6. Problem Solving

Example: | A greengrocer had **20** apples. If Johnny bought **30%** of the apples, how many apples did he buy? |

This is a two-step percentage problem.

Step 1 - First, find **10%** by dividing by **10**

$$20 ÷ 10 = 2 \text{ apples}$$

Step 2 - Then, find **30%** by multiplying by **3**

$$2 × 3 = 6 \text{ apples}$$

Answer: **6 apples**

Exercise 12: 8   Answer the following:

1) Richard saves **10%** on a laptop that originally cost **£200**. How much does he save? _____

2) Marlene has lost **20%** of her pens. She had **20** at the start. How many pens did she lose? _____

3) There are **350ml** of squash in a glass. William drinks **50%** of the squash. How much did he drink? _____

4) Charley collects **4** out of **5** special trading cards. What percentage of special trading cards does she have? _____

5) In a tray of **16** cans, **25%** are damaged. How many are undamaged? _____

6) In Mr Holt's class of **28** children, **75%** of children get above **85%** in a test. How many children get above **85%**? _____

7) The price of a **£5** ticket goes up by **2%**. How much does it increase by? _____

8) Alicia runs **70%** of a **500m** race and Jada runs the rest. How far does Alicia run? _____

9) Aleah needs **70%** to pass an exam. If there are **120** questions, how many questions does she need to get correct to pass? _____

10) Grant has **180** marbles. He gives **20%** of the marbles to Gavin. How many marbles did he give to Gavin? _____

Chapter Thirteen
PROBABILITY
1. What is Probability?

Probability is a way of measuring how **likely** something is to happen.

This happening is called an **event** or **outcome**. An event that has not yet happened is a **possibility**.

Some probabilities cannot be measured exactly. They can range from **definite (certain)** through to **impossible**, as in the following examples.

Certain	The sun will rise tomorrow.
↑	
Likely	I will have three meals today.
↑	
Possible	It will rain tomorrow.
↑	
Unlikely	I will win the lottery jackpot.
↑	
Impossible	I will fly to Mars next week.

Example: What is the probability that the moon will be seen in the sky again? Choose from:

certain   likely   possible   unlikely   impossible

Although the moon cannot be seen every night, it is certain that the moon will be seen again.

Answer: **certain**

Exercise 13: 1

Write if the event is certain, likely, possible, unlikely or impossible:

1) A volcano will erupt in England next week. _____

2) I will go to sleep tonight. _____

3) Spring follows summer. _____

4) It will be very windy tomorrow. _____

5) Monday is before Tuesday. _____

6) There are **7** days in a week. _____

7) I will be struck by lightning next week. _____

8) I will meet the Prime Minister within the next month. _____

9) At least **one** person in my class will have a birthday this week. _____

10) Christmas will be on **26ᵗʰ December** this year. _____

2. Equal Probabilities

It is possible to exactly measure probability when all the possible results have the same chance of happening. This means **all the probabilities are equal**.

Objects that give **Equal Probabilities** are described as **fair** as each outcome is equally likely.

This applies to objects such as dice, spinners, coins and playing cards.

Dice

6 equal shaped sides. There is an equal chance of throwing a **1**, **2**, **3**, **4**, **5** or **6**.

A Spinner

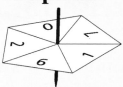

5 equal shaped sides. Each face is equally likely to be landed on.

A Coin

2 equal sides. There is an equal chance of tossing a head or a tail.

Playing Cards

52 cards that look identical when face down. Choosing any card is equally likely.

An object is **unfair** or **biased** if it does **not** give equally likely outcomes.

For example, a fake coin with tails on both sides would not be a fair coin.

Same coin

Example: | If five cards from the suit of hearts are removed from a pack of playing cards, is it a fair or unfair pack?

There are **four** suits in a complete pack of **52** playing cards: hearts, diamonds, spades and clubs. Each suit should have **13** cards in it. It is an unfair pack because there is no longer an equal chance of selecting a heart, diamond, spade or club. This pack no longer has equal probability.

Answer: **unfair**

Exercise 13: 2

Does the event have equal probability? Write yes or no:

1) A normal **6-sided** die. _____

2) An incomplete pack of playing cards. _____

3) A normal **10p** coin. _____

4) A complete pack of **52** playing cards. _____

5) A spinner with **5** sections numbered **1**, **2**, **2**, **3**, **4**. _____

Write whether the following are fair or unfair:

6) A weighted die so that one number is more likely. _____

7) The toss of a double-headed coin. _____

8) A spinner with **5** equal sections. _____

9) Picking a card from an incomplete set of **35** playing cards. _____

10) A normal **6-sided** die. _____

3. Possible Outcomes

An **Outcome** is the **result** of an activity or event.

For example, when a die is rolled, this is called the event. It can land on a **1**, **2**, **3**, **4**, **5** or **6** and these numbers are the **set of all possible outcomes**.

A set of all possible outcomes can be listed for any object that give equal probabilities.

Example: What are all the possible outcomes if a fair **5p** coin is tossed?

A fair coin that is tossed fairly only gives two possible outcomes: **heads** or **tails**. This means that heads and tails is the set of all possible outcomes.

Answer: **heads and tails**

Exercise 13: 3

Write out the possible outcomes:

Score

1) Which of the main directions a compass needle could point to. _____ _____ _____ _____

2) Which hand you write with. _____ _____

3) A multiple-choice question with options A to D.

_____ _____ _____ _____

4) A die with odd and even numbers on it.

_____ _____

5) A spinner with **4** coloured sections: red, blue, green and yellow. _____ _____ _____ _____

6) A bag containing **five** different coloured balls: red, blue, green, yellow and white.

_____ _____ _____ _____ _____

7) Silver coins that could be in your purse.

_____ _____ _____ _____

8) Toss of a fair coin. _____ _____

9) Suits in a set of playing cards.

_____ _____ _____ _____

10) A fair die. _____ _____ _____ _____ _____ _____

4. Calculating Probability

Probabilities that can be exactly calculated can be written as fractions as follows:

$$\text{Probability} = \frac{\textbf{Number of Results}}{\textbf{Number of Possible Results}}$$

- The numerator of the fraction shows how many times the event can occur.
- The denominator shows how many possible outcomes there could be.

For example, the probability of selecting a white ball from this bag can be written as:

Selecting a white ball can only occur **five** times; the numerator is **5**.

There are **ten** possible outcomes (**ten** balls); the denominator is **10**.

$$\frac{\circ\circ\circ\circ\circ}{\bullet\bullet\bullet\bullet\bullet} = \frac{\cancel{5}^{\,1}}{\cancel{10}^{\,2}} = \frac{1}{2}$$

Simplify (divide by **5**)

This can be called a **1** in **2** chance.

Example: | What is the probability of throwing a **1**, **2**, **3** or **4** when rolling a die?

Step 1 - List the results asked for in the question.

      1, **2**, **3** or **4** (**four** in total)

Step 2 - List all of the possible results.

      1, **2**, **3**, **4**, **5** or **6** (**six** in total)

Step 3 - Place these amounts into the fraction.

$$\frac{\textbf{Number of Results}}{\textbf{Number of Possible Results}} = \frac{4}{6}$$

Step 4 - Simplify the fraction:

Divide by **2**

$$\frac{\cancel{4}^{\,2}}{\cancel{6}^{\,3}} = \frac{2}{3}$$

Answer: $\frac{2}{3}$ or **a 2 in 3 chance**

Exercise 13: 4   Answer the following:

Score

1) What is the probability of picking a white ball out of **5** different coloured balls? ____

2) What is the probability of choosing the winning ticket out of **5** tickets? ____

3) What is the probability of rolling a **6** on a fair die? ____

4) What is the probability of picking one card out of a **52-pack** of playing cards? ____

5) What is the probability of landing a **4** on a fair **5-sided** spinner numbered **1-5**? ____

6) What is the probability of choosing a **two** out of a pack of **52** playing cards? ____

7) What is the probability of rolling an odd number on a fair die? ____

8) On a spinner with **2** green sections, **2** yellow sections and **2** red sections, what is the probability of landing on a yellow section? ____

9) If **10** raffle tickets win out of **15** tickets sold, what is the chance of winning the prize? ____

10) What is the probability of rolling a **2**, **3**, or **5** on a fair die? ____

5. Problem Solving

Example: Tracey's school is holding a raffle at the school fête. **30** tickets have been sold. There is a **1** in **10** chance that Tracey will win first prize. How many raffle tickets has Tracey bought?

A **1** in **10** chance is the same as finding **one-tenth**.

To find $\frac{1}{10}$ of **30**, divide **30** by **10**.

$$30 \div 10 = 3$$

The **30** tickets are shown in the diagram below:

$$\frac{1}{10} \text{ of } \textbf{30} = \textbf{3}$$

Answer: **3 tickets**

Exercise 13: 5   Answer the following:

1) **One** sweet is picked at random from a bag containing **7** chocolates and **3** mints. What is the probability of picking a chocolate? _____

2) There is a **1** in **5** chance that Andrew will win a prize in the raffle. If **30** tickets were sold, how many tickets does Andrew have? _____

3) In a class of **10** boys and **10** girls, what is the chance of picking a girl to answer a question? _____

4) In a pack of pens there are **3** black pens, **3** blue pens, **3** red pens and **2** green pens. What is the probability of picking a blue pen? _____

5) **One** card is drawn at random from an ordinary pack of **52** playing cards. What is the probability of picking a red card? _____

6) If there is a $\frac{7}{10}$ chance of picking a winning ticket, what is the probability a winning ticket will not be picked? _____

7) Debbie needs to roll a **5** to win the game. If she uses a fair die, what is the probability of rolling a **5**? _____

8) On a dessert menu there are **15** items. **10** items have ice cream in them. What is the probability of ordering something at random with ice cream in it? _____

9) Harriet buys **80** tickets out of **100**. What is the chance of her winning the raffle? _____

10) A spinner has **7** equal sections numbered **1-7**. What is the probability of the spinner landing on the number **5**? _____

Chapter Fourteen
LINES & ANGLES
1. Types of Line

A **Line** joins two points together. Lines can be straight or curved, as shown below:

Straight   **Curved**

Lines can be described in the following ways:

Horizontal • Vertical • Diagonal
Parallel • Perpendicular

a. Horizontal, Vertical & Diagonal

Vertical Lines

A line drawn straight 'up' or 'down' or exactly upright.

Horizontal Lines

A line drawn straight 'across' flat like the horizon.

Diagonal Lines

A straight line that slants is a **diagonal**. Any straight line that is not horizontal or vertical is diagonal.

Example: | Is this line horizontal, vertical or diagonal?

The line is not exactly upright or drawn straight across, so it must be a diagonal line.

Answer: **diagonal**

Exercise 14: 1 Answer the following:

Score

a   b   c ——— d

e   f   g ——— h

1) Is **a** horizontal, vertical or diagonal? _____

2) Is **c** horizontal, vertical or diagonal? _____

3) Is **f** horizontal, vertical or diagonal? _____

4) Which two lines are horizontal? _____ and _____

5) Which three lines are diagonal? _____, _____ and _____

6) How many diagonal lines
   are in this picture? ____

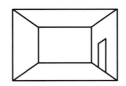

7) How many vertical lines
   are in this picture? ____

8) How many vertical lines
   are in this picture? ____

9) How many diagonal lines
   are in this picture? ____

10) How many horizontal lines
    are in this picture? ____

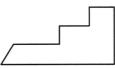

b. Parallel & Perpendicular

Parallel Lines

Lines that always stay the same distance apart and never meet are **parallel**.

Arrows can be used to show the lines are parallel. Parallel lines can be straight or curved.

Perpendicular Lines

When a horizontal line meets a vertical line the two lines are **perpendicular** to each other.

Example: | Are these lines parallel or perpendicular?

These lines are the same distance apart and do not meet. They must be parallel lines.

Answer: **parallel**

Exercise 14: 2 Answer the following:

Score

a ═══ b ┼ c └ d ⫽ e ≈

f ‖ g ⌐ h ⊤ i ⊢ j ≈

1) Is **a** parallel or perpendicular? _____

2) Is **d** parallel or perpendicular? _____

3) Is **g** parallel or perpendicular? _____

4) Is **i** parallel or perpendicular? _____

5) Is **b** parallel or perpendicular? _____

6) Is **f** parallel or perpendicular? _____

7) Is **c** parallel or perpendicular? _____

8) Is **h** parallel or perpendicular? _____

9) Which lines are parallel? _____

10) Which lines are perpendicular? _____

c. Mixed Line Questions

Exercise 14: 3   Answer the following:

Score

1) Two sides of a trapezium are _____ .
   (vertical, parallel, perpendicular)

2) The floor and ceiling of a room are _____ .
   (vertical, perpendicular, parallel)

3) The sides of a ladder are _____ to each other.
   (parallel, horizontal, perpendicular)

4) Sides **a** & **b** of this square are

_____ to each other.

(vertical, parallel, perpendicular)

a

b

5) Two sides of the parallelogram are

_____ .

(vertical, diagonal, perpendicular)

6) Are these lines parallel or perpendicular?

_____ .

7) The walls of a room are _____ .

(vertical, horizontal, perpendicular)

8) A lamppost is _____ .

(vertical, parallel, horizontal)

9) The pavement is _____ to the road.

(diagonal, perpendicular, parallel)

10) Is this line vertical, horizontal or diagonal? ———

_____ .

2. Types of Angle

Angles are formed when two straight lines meet.

Angles are measured in degrees.

The degrees symbol is °.

A curved line is used between the two straight lines to show an angle.

?°

a. Right Angles & Straight Lines

A **Right Angle** equals **90°** and is the same as the corner of a square, rectangle or a piece of paper. It is shown using a box symbol in the corner of the angle, like this:

A **Straight Line** equals **180°** and is formed from two right angles.

Right Angle
90°

Straight Line
180°

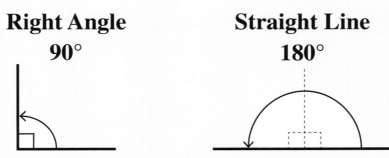

Example: | Mark the right angles in this shape.

A right angle would form the corner of a square and looks like this:

This shape has **four** angles.

Angles **1** and **3** are larger than a right angle.

Angle **2** is smaller than a right angle.

Angle **4** is a right angle and the box is marked in that angle.

4

1 ⌒ **3**

2

Answer:

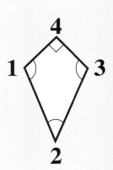

Exercise 14: 4

Mark all of the right angles on the inside and outside of the shape:

1)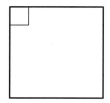

2)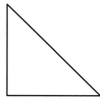

3)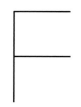

4)

5)

6)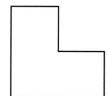

7)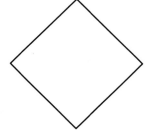

8)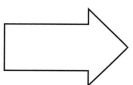

9)

10)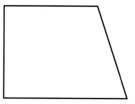

Example: Does this object have any right angles in real life?

This microwave is shaped like a box and therefore will have many right angles.

Answer: **yes**

Exercise 14: 5

Does the object have any right angles in real life? Write yes or no.

Score

1)

_____

2)

_____

3)

_____

4)

_____

5)

_____

6)

_____

7)

_____

8)

_____

9)

_____

10)

_____

b. Right Angles in a Full Circle

The diagrams show a line as it turns through **4** right angles to complete a full turn of **360°**.

A $\frac{1}{4}$ turn	A $\frac{1}{2}$ turn	A $\frac{3}{4}$ turn	A full turn
90°	180°	270°	360°
	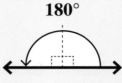	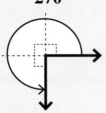	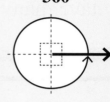
1 right angle	**2** right angles	**3** right angles	**4** right angles

---

Example: ┃ How many degrees are in a **half** turn? ┃

A half turn is the same as two right angles.

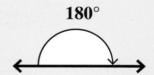

$$90° + 90° = 180°$$

Answer: **180°**

Exercise 14: 6   Answer the following:

1) How many right angles are in **1** full turn? _____

2) How many right angles are in a $\frac{1}{2}$ turn? _____

3) How many right angles are in a $\frac{1}{4}$ turn? _____

4) How many right angles are in a $\frac{3}{4}$ turn? _____

5) How many right angles are in **2** full turns? _____

6) What is a $\frac{1}{2}$ turn in degrees? _____

7) What is a $\frac{3}{4}$ turn in degrees? _____

8) What is **1** full turn in degrees? _____

9) What is a $\frac{1}{4}$ turn in degrees? _____

10) What is a **1$\frac{1}{2}$** turn in degrees? _____

Score

c. Acute, Obtuse & Reflex Angles

Angles that are not right angles or straight lines can be split into three types:

> 1. **Acute**   2. **Obtuse**   3. **Reflex**

Acute angles can be called 'narrow' angles and obtuse and reflex angles can be called 'wide' angles.

1. **Acute - Up to 90°**
An acute angle is any angle that is less than **90°**.

2. **Obtuse - Above 90° to 180°**
An obtuse angle is bigger than **90°** but less than **180°**.

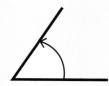

3. **Reflex - Above 180° to 360°**
A reflex angle is bigger than **180°** but less than **360°**. These angles are both reflex angles but look very different from each other.

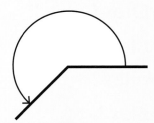

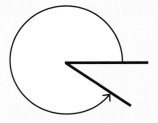

Example: Is this angle acute, obtuse or reflex?

If this angle is compared with a right angle, it can be seen that it is more than **90°** but less than **180°** and is obtuse.

Example Angle   **Right Angle**

Answer: **obtuse**

Exercise 14: 7   Answer the following:

Score

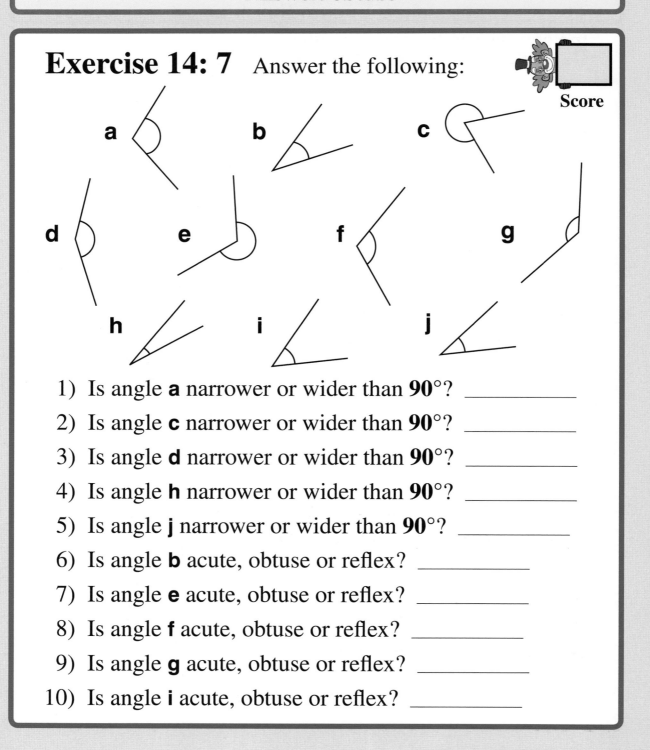

1) Is angle **a** narrower or wider than **90°**? _____

2) Is angle **c** narrower or wider than **90°**? _____

3) Is angle **d** narrower or wider than **90°**? _____

4) Is angle **h** narrower or wider than **90°**? _____

5) Is angle **j** narrower or wider than **90°**? _____

6) Is angle **b** acute, obtuse or reflex? _____

7) Is angle **e** acute, obtuse or reflex? _____

8) Is angle **f** acute, obtuse or reflex? _____

9) Is angle **g** acute, obtuse or reflex? _____

10) Is angle **i** acute, obtuse or reflex? _____

3. Compass Directions
a. The Compass Points

A **Compass** is an instrument used to find direction. The compass needle is magnetic and will always point north. All other directions can be found by measuring from north.

There are four main **Compass Directions**. A full turn of the compass is four right angles.

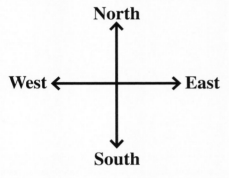

A way to remember the compass points going right around the circle is:

Naughty
Elephants
Squirt
Water

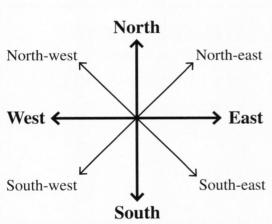

There are four more compass points. Each one is halfway between each main compass point. For example, halfway between north and east is north-east.

Example: | Which compass point is halfway between south and west?

The diagram shows that the compass point south-west is between south and west.

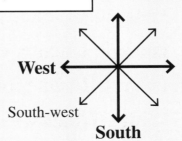

Answer: **south-west**

Exercise 14: 8a   Answer the following:

1) Fill in the missing compass directions.

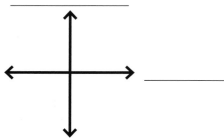

Where is the needle pointing?

2)    3)    4)    5)

b. Clockwise & Anticlockwise

If a person is using a compass, they often have to change direction. This means turning left or right.

Right-hand turns using a compass are **Clockwise** (as the clock goes) and left-hand turns are **Anticlockwise**.

Clockwise Anticlockwise

A useful way to remember clockwise and anticlockwise is that bottle tops are tightened clockwise and loosened anticlockwise.

   **Right-hand turn**
Clockwise

   **Left-hand turn**
Anticlockwise

Example: If Charlie was facing west and turned a **quarter** turn anticlockwise, in what direction would he now be facing?

Charlie turned anticlockwise which means he turned to the left.
A **quarter** turn is a right angle.
The diagram shows Charlie now faces south.

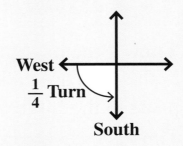

Answer: **south**

Exercise 14: 8b   Answer the following:

6) If the needle is pointing north and turns a $\frac{3}{4}$ turn in a clockwise direction, where is it pointing? _____

7) If the needle is pointing south-east and turns a $\frac{1}{2}$ turn in an anticlockwise direction, where is it pointing?

_____

8) If the needle is pointing north-west and turns a $\frac{1}{4}$ turn in a clockwise direction, where is it pointing?

_____

9) If the needle is pointing west and turns a $\frac{3}{4}$ turn in an anticlockwise direction, where is it pointing?

_____

10) If the needle is pointing north-east, and turns a $\frac{1}{4}$ turn in a clockwise direction, where is it pointing? _____

Chapter Fifteen
TIME
1. Time Measurement

Time is the ongoing series of events that have taken place in the past, are taking place in the present, and will take place in the future.

Time is measured using seconds, minutes, hours, days, weeks, months and years.

a. Years

A **Year** is the amount of time it takes the Earth to move in a full circle around the Sun. This takes **365 and one-quarter** days.

This is awkward for counting days, so every **4** years an extra day is added to make a **leap year** of **366** days.

For example, **2008**, **2012** and **2016** were leap years.

The basic measurements for time periods are shown below:

1 decade	= **10** years
365 days	= **1** year
366 days	= **1** leap year
12 months	= **1** year
52 weeks	= **1** year

Example: | How many years are there in **2** decades?

There are **10** years in **1** decade, so this needs to be multiplied by **2**.

$$10 \text{ years} \times 2 = 20 \text{ years}$$

Answer: **20 years**

Exercise 15: 1 Answer the following:

1) How many days are in **2** years (no leap years)? _____

2) Was **1990** a leap year? _____

3) Leap years happen every _____ years.

4) How many weeks are there in **3** years? _____

5) **Four** decades is _____ years.

6) How many days are there in a leap year? _____

7) A year is _____ weeks.

8) How many days are there in **3** weeks? _____

9) How many months are there in **2** years? _____

10) How many days are there in **4** weeks? _____

Score

b. Months

The year is divided into **12 Months**. Each month is roughly **4 weeks**. The number of days in each month are as follows:

January	**31** days
February	**28/29** days
March	**31** days
April	**30** days
May	**31** days
June	**30** days
July	**31** days
August	**31** days
September	**30** days
October	**31** days
November	**30** days
December	**31** days

Knowing the number of days in each month is really important. This rhyme is a good way of learning this:

30 days have September, April, June and November. All the rest have **31**, except February alone which has **28** days clear, but **29** in each leap year.

Note: **4** months have **30** days
7 months have **31** days
1 month has **28/29** days

Exercise 15: 2

Put the months in order by matching the month to the correct number:

November ● --------- ● 7

July ● --------- ● 3

1) March ● ● 10

2) January ● ● 8

3) September ● ● 5

4) May ● ● 1

5) December ● ● 2

6) August ● ● 11

7) February ● ● 4

8) October ● ● 9

9) June ● ● 12

10) April ● ● 6

Score

Exercise 15: 3 Write the months in order:

Score

1) The first month is _____

2) The second month is _____

3) The third month is _____

4) The fourth month is _____

The fifth month is ___May___

5) The sixth month is _____

The seventh month is ___July___

6) The eighth month is _____

7) The ninth month is _____

8) The tenth month is _____

9) The eleventh month is _____

10) The twelfth month is _____

Exercise 15: 4 Which month is:

Score

1) **three** months before October? _____

2) between July and September? _____

3) **two** months after December? _____

4) **six** months before November? _____

5) between February and April? _____

6) **two** months after November? _____

7) between October and December? _____

How many months are there before:

8) May? _____   9) April? _____

10) July? _____

Exercise 15: 5

Match the month to the correct number of days in that month:

	Month		Days
	May		30
	April		31
1)	July		31
2)	February		30
3)	October		28
4)	January		31
5)	November		31
6)	June		31
7)	September		30
8)	December		31
9)	August		31
10)	March		30

Score

c. Weeks

There are **7** days in a **Week**.
A week begins on a Monday and
ends on a Sunday.
Two weeks are called a fortnight.

| Monday |
| Tuesday |
| Wednesday |
| Thursday |
| Friday |
| Saturday |
| Sunday |

1 week   = **7** days
1 fortnight = **14** days
1 weekend = Saturday & Sunday

The working week is Monday-Friday. Some countries view
Sunday as the first day of the week instead of Monday.

Score

Exercise 15: 6 Answer the following:

1) Which two days make up the weekend?

   _____ and _____

2) How many times will Tuesday appear in a
   fortnight? _____

Which day is:

3) **two** days after Thursday? _____

4) between Monday and Wednesday? _____

5) **three** days before Wednesday? _____

6) **three** days after Monday? _____

7) **four** days before Sunday? _____

8) between Thursday and Saturday? _____

9) **two** days before Tuesday? _____

10) between Sunday and Tuesday? _____

2. Dates

Any day in any year is described using a **Date**. This can be written in full or in figures.

For example, the **second** day of **June** in **2014** can be written in the following ways:

In full	In figures
2nd June 2014	02.06.14

When writing dates in full and in figures the order is always day, month, year.

In figures, the year is often shortened to the last two digits but can be written using four digits such as **02.06.2014**.

The day, month and year are separated by full stops or forward slashes, for example **02/06/14**.

a. In Figures

Example: How would the date **7th September 2015** be written in figures?

When writing this date in figures it should follow the order of day, month and year.

The **7th** day of the month will be written as **07**.

September is the **ninth** month so it will be written as **09**.

2015 will usually be shortened to **15**, but it can also be written as **2015**.

Answer: **07.09.15**

Exercise 15: 7   Write the date in figures:

1) **8th June 1967** _____

2) **22nd September 1996** _____

3) **1st April 1980** _____

4) **14th February 2015** _____

5) **31st December 2002** _____

6) **28th July 1973** _____

7) **21st January 1970** _____

8) **4th August 1987** _____

9) **19th March 2008** _____

10) **3rd May 2013** _____

Score

b. In Full

Example: | How would the date **16.05.04** be written in full?

When writing this date in full it should follow the order of day, month and year.

16 will be written as the **16th** day.

05 is the **fifth** month so it will be **May**.

04 represents the year **2004**.

Answer: **16th May 2004**

Exercise 15: 8   Write the date in full:

1) **08/11/2015** _____

2) **10.10.1996** _____

3) **05.02.62** _____

4) **04/06/11** _____

5) **27.06.97** _____

6) **20.08.1962** _____

7) **29/02/16** _____

8) **20.04.54** _____

9) **11/05/1994** _____

10) **27.12.65** _____

Score

c. The Calendar

The **Calendar** is a diagram that shows what day, month and year it is. A full calendar will show all **365/366** days split over **12** months.

A new calendar is created every year. It shows which day of the week each date falls on, as this changes every year.

Calendars can show each week beginning on Monday or Sunday, so it is important to read the calendar carefully.

The days of the week are often shortened to one or two letters as shown below:

M	Tu	W	Th	F	Sa	Su
Monday	Tuesday	Wednesday	Thursday	Friday	Saturday	Sunday

Example: | What day of the week is **17ᵗʰ April**?

Look along the rows (go left or right) for the number **17** on the calendar.

See which column (go up or down) **17** is in.

In this April calendar, the number **17** is in the 'Friday' column.

April						
M	Tu	W	Th	F	Sa	Su
		1	2	3	4	5
6	7	8	9	10	11	12
13	14	15	16	17	18	19
20	21	22	23	24	25	26
27	28	29	30			

Answer: **Friday**

Exercise 15: 9

Answer the following (include the day of the week if required):

Score

January

Su	M	Tu	W	Th	F	Sa
1	2	3	4	5	6	7
8	9	10	11	12	13	14
15	16	17	18	19	20	21
22	23	24	25	26	27	28
29	30	31				

1) What day of the week is **28ᵗʰ January**? _____

2) How many days from Monday **9ᵗʰ** to the next Monday? _____

3) What is the date a week after **5ᵗʰ January**? _____

4) How many Sundays are in this month? _____

5) What date is the **fourth** Tuesday? _____

June

M	Tu	W	Th	F	Sa	Su
			1	2	3	4
5	6	7	8	9	10	11
12	13	14	15	16	17	18
19	20	21	22	23	24	25
26	27	28	29	30		

6) How many Mondays are in this month? _____

7) What date is the **second** Friday? _____

8) How many days from Thursday **22ⁿᵈ** to the next Thursday? _____

9) What day of the week is **25ᵗʰ June**? _____

10) What is the date a week after **13ᵗʰ June**? _____

Example: | What is the date of the next Tuesday after **29ᵗʰ September 2015**?

2015 Calendar

September

Su	M	Tu	W	Th	F	Sa
		1	2	3	4	5
6	7	8	9	10	11	12
13	14	15	16	17	18	19
20	21	22	23	24	25	26
27	28	(29)	30			

October

Su	M	Tu	W	Th	F	Sa
				1	2	3
4	5	(6)	7	8	9	10
11	12	13	14	15	16	17
18	19	20	21	22	23	24
25	26	27	28	29	30	31

November

Su	M	Tu	W	Th	F	Sa
1	2	3	4	5	6	7
8	9	10	11	12	13	14
15	16	17	18	19	20	21
22	23	24	25	26	27	28
29	30					

Notice that this calendar starts the week on a Sunday.

Find **Tuesday 29ᵗʰ September 2015** on the calendar by looking down the columns and along the rows.

The next Tuesday is in October. The first time a Tuesday appears in October 2015 is **Tuesday 6ᵗʰ October 2015**.

Answer: **Tuesday 6ᵗʰ October 2015**

Exercise 15: 10

Answer the following (include the day of the week if required):

2016 Calendar

January

M	Tu	W	Th	F	Sa	Su
				1	2	3
4	5	6	7	8	9	10
11	12	13	14	15	16	17
18	19	20	21	22	23	24
25	26	27	28	29	30	31

February

M	Tu	W	Th	F	Sa	Su
1	2	3	4	5	6	7
8	9	10	11	12	13	14
15	16	17	18	19	20	21
22	23	24	25	26	27	28
29						

March

M	Tu	W	Th	F	Sa	Su
	1	2	3	4	5	6
7	8	9	10	11	12	13
14	15	16	17	18	19	20
21	22	23	24	25	26	27
28	29	30	31			

April

M	Tu	W	Th	F	Sa	Su
				1	2	3
4	5	6	7	8	9	10
11	12	13	14	15	16	17
18	19	20	21	22	23	24
25	26	27	28	29	30	

May

M	Tu	W	Th	F	Sa	Su
						1
2	3	4	5	6	7	8
9	10	11	12	13	14	15
16	17	18	19	20	21	22
23	24	25	26	27	28	29
30	31					

June

M	Tu	W	Th	F	Sa	Su
		1	2	3	4	5
6	7	8	9	10	11	12
13	14	15	16	17	18	19
20	21	22	23	24	25	26
27	28	29	30			

July

M	Tu	W	Th	F	Sa	Su
				1	2	3
4	5	6	7	8	9	10
11	12	13	14	15	16	17
18	19	20	21	22	23	24
25	26	27	28	29	30	31

August

M	Tu	W	Th	F	Sa	Su
1	2	3	4	5	6	7
8	9	10	11	12	13	14
15	16	17	18	19	20	21
22	23	24	25	26	27	28
29	30	31				

September

M	Tu	W	Th	F	Sa	Su
			1	2	3	4
5	6	7	8	9	10	11
12	13	14	15	16	17	18
19	20	21	22	23	24	25
26	27	28	29	30		

October

M	Tu	W	Th	F	Sa	Su
					1	2
3	4	5	6	7	8	9
10	11	12	13	14	15	16
17	18	19	20	21	22	23
24	25	26	27	28	29	30
31						

November

M	Tu	W	Th	F	Sa	Su
	1	2	3	4	5	6
7	8	9	10	11	12	13
14	15	16	17	18	19	20
21	22	23	24	25	26	27
28	29	30				

December

M	Tu	W	Th	F	Sa	Su
			1	2	3	4
5	6	7	8	9	10	11
12	13	14	15	16	17	18
19	20	21	22	23	24	25
26	27	28	29	30	31	

1) What day of the week is **7ᵗʰ August 2016**? _____

2) What is the date of the next Saturday after **3ʳᵈ July 2016**? _____

3) What is the date a week after **2ⁿᵈ September**?

    _____

4) How many Sundays are there in **January 2016**? _____

5) What date is the **third** Wednesday in **March 2016**?

    _____

6) What day of the week is **17ᵗʰ November 2016**?

    _____

7) What date is the **second** Wednesday in **September 2016**? _____

8) What is the date of the next Tuesday after **30ᵗʰ August 2016**? _____

9) What day of the week is **27ᵗʰ June 2016**? _____

10) What is the date of the next Friday after **26ᵗʰ February 2016**? _____

Score

3. The Analogue Clock

Clocks are used to tell what time of the day it is. Clocks measure hours, minutes and seconds.

Clocks that have hands or pointers are called **Analogue Clocks**.

There are **24** hours in a day. The clock shows **12** hours, so in a full day the clock will show each time twice.

Clock time measures seconds, minutes, hours and days.
The basic measurements of time are shown below:

> 1 minute (mins) = **60** seconds (secs)
> 1 hour (hrs)   = **60** minutes
> 1 day   = **24** hours

Example: | How many minutes are there in $1\frac{1}{4}$ hours?

There are **60** minutes in **1** hour.

$\frac{1}{4}$ of an hour is **15** minutes, because **60 ÷ 4 = 15**.

60 minutes + **15** minutes = **75** minutes

Answer: **75 minutes**

Exercise 15: 11 Answer the following:

How many minutes are there in:

1) **2** hours = _____ mins   2) **3** hours = _____ mins

3) $4\frac{1}{2}$ hours = _____ mins

Convert to hours and minutes:

4) **87mins** = __ hr __ mins 5) **103mins** = __ hr __ mins

How many seconds are there in:

6) $1\frac{1}{2}$**mins**? _____ secs   7) **4mins**? _____ secs

8) **5mins**? _____ secs

Convert to minutes and seconds:

9) **72** seconds = _____ mins _____ secs

10) **143** seconds = _____ mins _____ secs

Score

a. The Clock Face

The **Clock Face** shows time in hours and minutes. The numbers on the inside show which hour of the day it is. There are **12** hours in total on the clock face.

The marks around the edge show the minutes of the hour. There are **60** minutes in total on the clock face.

The longer hand points to which minute of the hour it is.

The shorter hand points to which hour of the day it is.

The hands of the clock always move to the right in a circular motion or in a **clockwise** direction.

b. The Minute Hand

A clock face shows **60** minute markings around the edge.

The **Minute Hand** takes **60** minutes or **1** hour to circle the clock face.

There are **12** hour markings around the clock face. Each are **5** minutes apart.

This minute hand points to **2**, which is **10** minutes.

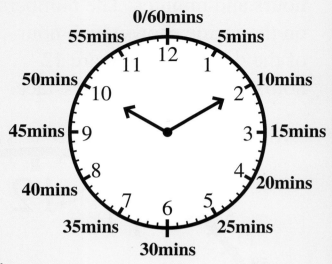

Example: How many minutes are in this section of the clock?

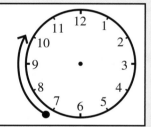

The arrows covers **three** sections of **5** minutes.

$$3 \times 5 \text{ minutes} = 15 \text{ minutes}$$

Answer: **15 minutes**

Exercise 15: 12 How many minutes are in this section of the clock?

Score

1) 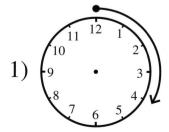 _____ 2)  _____

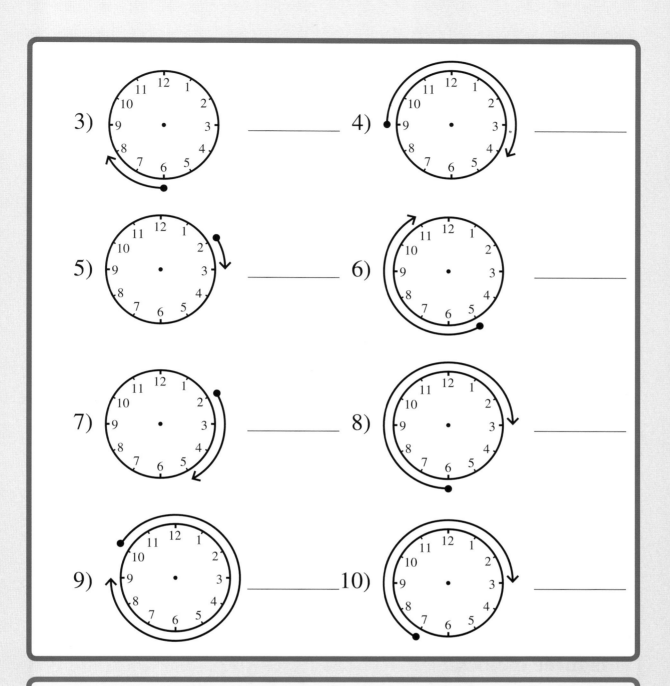

3) _____ 4) _____

5) _____ 6) _____

7) _____ 8) _____

9) _____ 10) _____

Times in Full & in Figures

Time can be written in two ways; in full and in figures.

For example, this clock shows **twenty minutes past 12**, which can also be written as **12.20**.

When time is written in figures, a full stop is used to separate the hours from the minutes.

c. O'clock (The Hour Hand)

When the time is exactly on the hour, it is called an **O'clock** time.

The hour hand points exactly to the number of the hour. The minute hand always points to **12** (or **0** minutes).

Times can be written in figures and in full. The time on this clock is exactly **ten o'clock** or **10.00** (**ten** hours and **zero** minutes).

It takes **12** hours for the hour hand to make a full circle around the clock face.

Example:
What time is shown on this clock? 

The minute (longer) hand points to **12**. This means it is an o'clock time.

The hour (shorter) hand points to **3**. This means the time is **three o'clock**.

Answer: **three o'clock** or **3.00**

Exercise 15: 13 What time is shown on the clock?

1)

Two o'clock

_____

2)

_____

8.00

3)

_____

_____

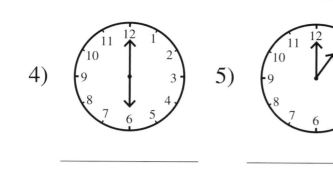

4) _____

_____

5) _____

_____

6) _____

_____

Draw the hands on the clock:

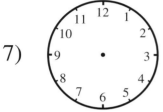

7) **Four o'clock**

8) **Seven o'clock**

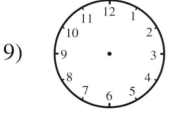

9) **Nine o'clock**

10) **Eleven o'clock**

Score

d. Quarter Past

The clock face can be split into four sections, called **quarters**.

Each **quarter** is **15** minutes, or a **quarter** of an hour.

This is because:

60 minutes ÷ **4** = **15** minutes

When it is **Quarter Past** the hour, the minute (longer) hand points to the number **3** (or **15** minutes). The hour (shorter) hand moves just beyond the number of hours.

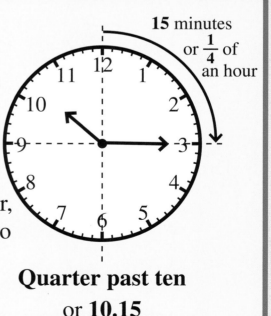

15 minutes or $\frac{1}{4}$ of an hour

Quarter past ten or **10.15**

Example: What time is shown on this clock?

The minute (longer) hand points to **3** (**15** minutes). This means it is a quarter past time.

The hour (shorter) hand points just beyond **7**. This means the time is **quarter past seven**.

Answer: **quarter past seven** or **7.15**

Exercise 15: 14 What time is shown on the clock?

1)

Quarter past eight

2)

2.15

3)

_____

4)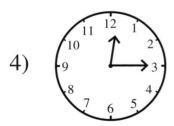

_____

5)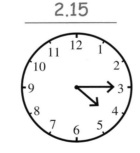

_____

6)

_____

Draw the hands on the clock:

7)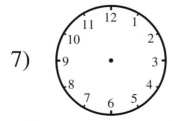

Quarter past nine

8)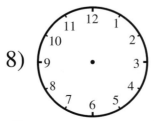

Quarter past six

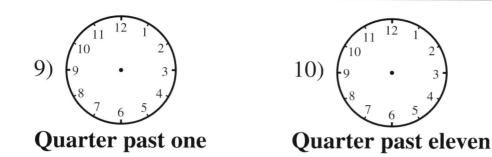

9) **Quarter past one**

10) **Quarter past eleven**

Score

e. Half Past

The clock face can be split into two sections, called **halves**.

Each **half** is **30** minutes, or **half** an hour.

This is because:

60 minutes ÷ **2** = **30** minutes

When it is **Half Past** the hour, the minute (longer) hand points to the number **6** (or **30** minutes). The hour (shorter) hand moves halfway between the number of hours.

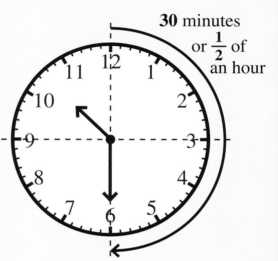

30 minutes or $\frac{1}{2}$ of an hour

Half past ten or **10.30**

Example: What time is shown on this clock?

The minute (longer) hand points to **6** (**30** minutes). This means it is a half past time.

The hour (shorter) hand points halfway between **4** and **5**. This means the time is **half past four**.

Answer: **half past four** or **4.30**

Exercise 15: 15 What time is shown on the clock?

1)

Half past one

2)

3.30

3)

_____

4)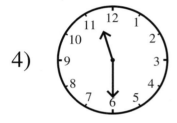

_____

_____

5)

_____

_____

6)

_____

_____

Draw the hands on the clock:

7)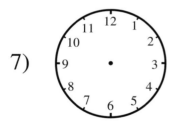

Half past two

8)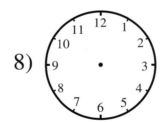

Half past five

9)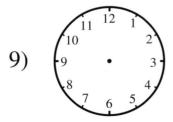

Half past nine

10)

Half past twelve

Score

ae

f. Quarter To

At the $\frac{3}{4}$ of an hour point on a clock, **45** minutes have passed.

This is because:

15mins × 3 = 45mins

When the minute (longer) hand points to the number **9** (or **45** minutes). The hour (shorter) hand almost reaches the next hour.

It is written as **Quarter To** the hour or as hours and minutes.

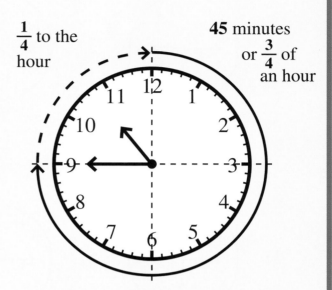

$\frac{1}{4}$ to the hour

45 minutes or $\frac{3}{4}$ of an hour

Quarter to eleven
or **10.45**

Example: What time is shown on this clock?

The minute (longer) hand points to **9** (**45** minutes). This means it is a quarter to time.

The hour (shorter) hand points to nearly **2**. This means the time is quarter to the next hour, which is **quarter to two**.

When writing this time in figures, it is written as **45** minutes past **1**, or **1.45**.

Answer: **quarter to two or 1.45**

Exercise 15: 16   What time is shown on the clock?

1)

Quarter to three

2)

7.45

3)

4)

5)

6)

Draw the hands on the clock:

7)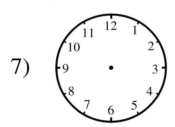

Quarter to four

8)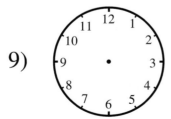

Quarter to seven

9)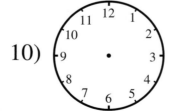

Quarter to ten

10)

Quarter to one

Score

g. Minutes Past the Hour

When the minute hand points from **1** minute to **30** minutes, the time is written as **Minutes Past the Hour**.

The most important are **5 past**, **10 past**, **15 past** (**quarter past**), **20 past**, **25 past** and **30 past** (**half past**).

When it is minutes past the hour, the minute (longer) hand points to the number of minutes. The hour (shorter) hand moves beyond the number of hours.

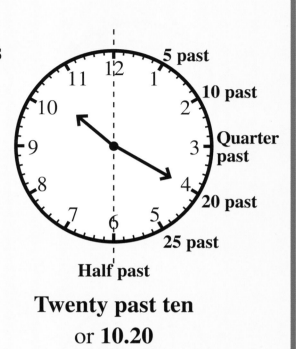

**Twenty past ten
or 10.20**

Example: | What time is shown on this clock, in full and in figures?

The minute (longer) hand points to **9** minutes. This means it is **9** minutes past the hour.

The hour (shorter) hand points just beyond **7**. This means the time is **nine minutes past seven**.

Answer: **nine minutes past seven** or **7.09**

Exercise 15: 17 What time is shown on the clock?

1)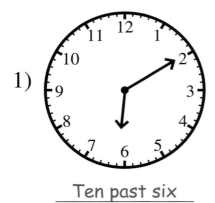

Ten past six

_____

2)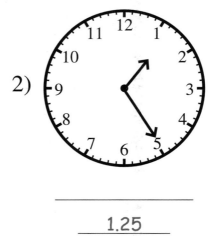

_____

_1.25_

3)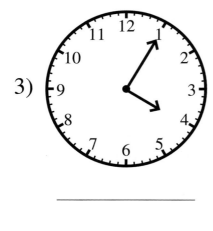

_____

_____

4)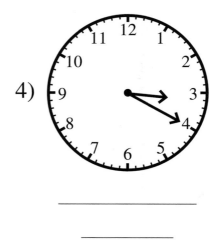

_____

_____

5)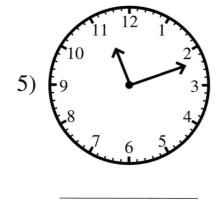

_____

_____

6)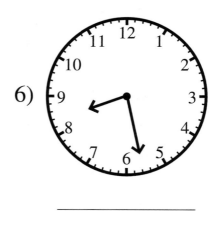

_____

_____

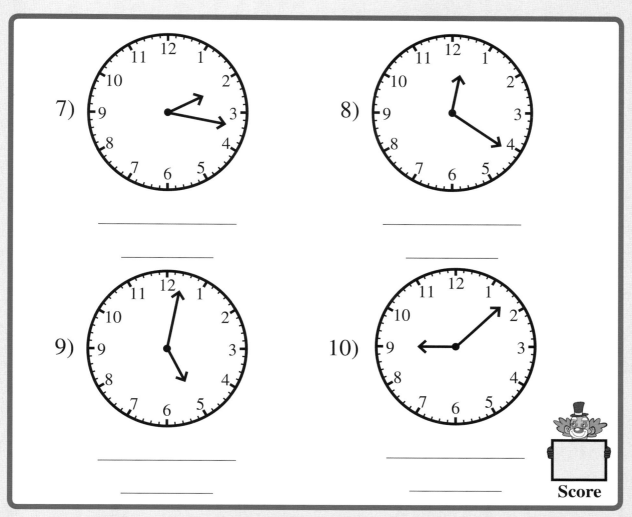

7) _____
   _____

8) _____
   _____

9) _____
   _____

10) _____
    _____

Score

h. Minutes to the Hour

When the minute hand points from **31** to **59** minutes, the time is written as **Minutes to the Hour**.

The most important times are **25 to**, **20 to**, **15 to (quarter to)**, **10 to** and **5 to**.

Minutes to the hour count the number of minutes left until the next hour begins.

The minute (longer) hand points to the number of minutes. The hour (shorter) hand moves closer to the next hour.

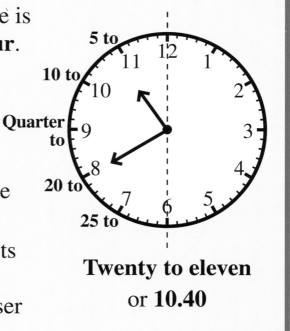

Twenty to eleven
or **10.40**

Example: What time is shown on this clock, in full and in figures?

The minute (longer) hand points to **53** minutes. This means it is **7** minutes to the next hour.

60mins – 53mins = 7mins

The hour (shorter) hand nearly reaches the number **4**.

This time in figures is written as **53** minutes past **3**, or **3.53**.

Answer: **seven minutes to four** or **3.53**

Exercise 15: 18 What time is shown on the clock?

1)

Five to two

_____

2)

_5.40_

_____

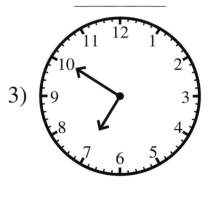

3)

_____

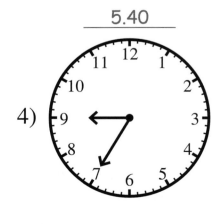

4)

_____

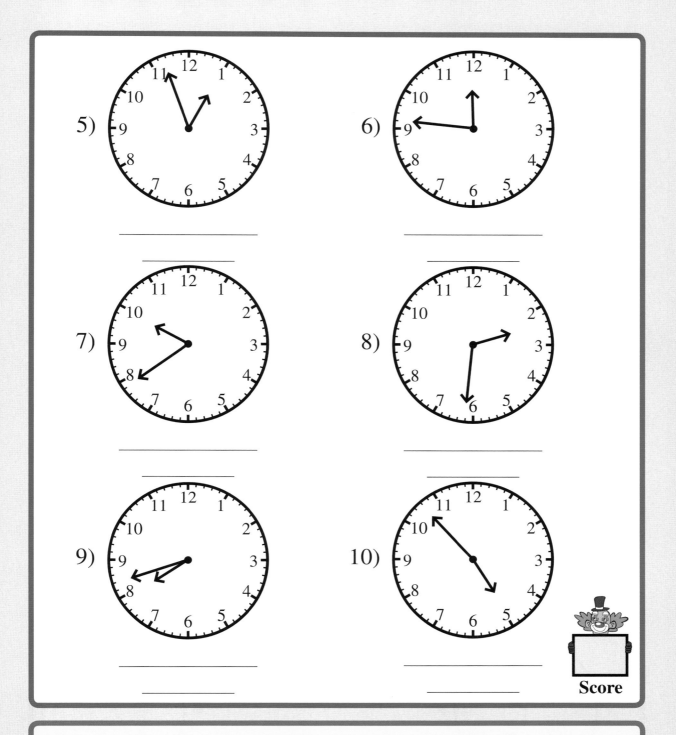

5) _____

6) _____

7) _____

8) _____

9) _____

10) _____

Score

Clocks can have different types of numbering. The layout is always the same; **12** at the top and **6** at the bottom.

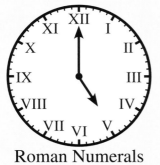

Roman Numerals

No Numbers

No Markings

i. Mixed Clock Face Questions

Exercise 15: 19   Match the clock face to the correct time:

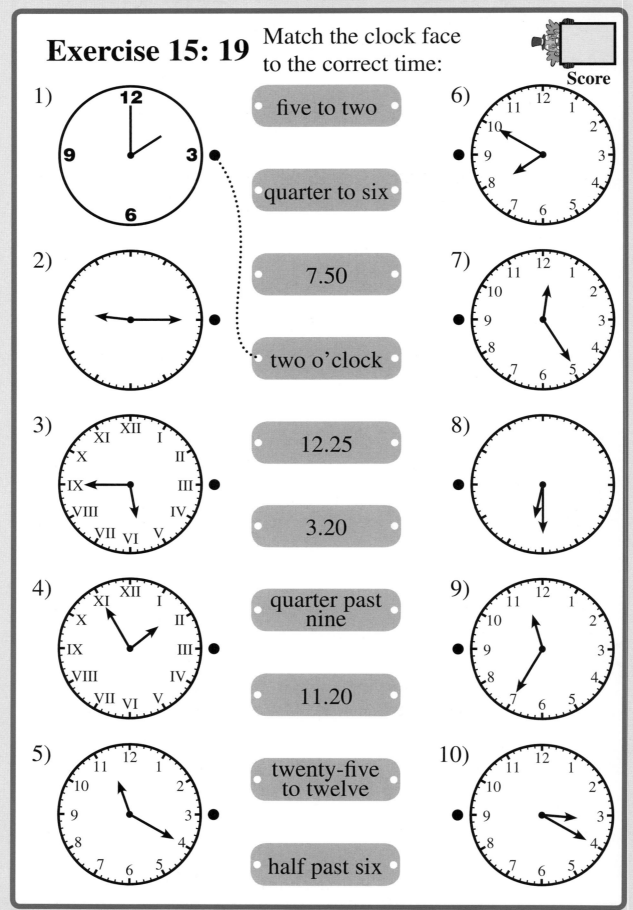

1)

five to two

quarter to six

7.50

two o'clock

12.25

3.20

quarter past nine

11.20

twenty-five to twelve

half past six

2)

3)

4)

5)

6)

7)

8)

9)

10)

4. 12-hour Time
a. The 12-hour System

There are **24** hours in a day. The first period is the morning and the second period is the afternoon and evening.

Written time must show whether it is morning or afternoon. Morning is written as 'am' and afternoon is 'pm'.

One day (**24** hours) is shown on the diagram below:

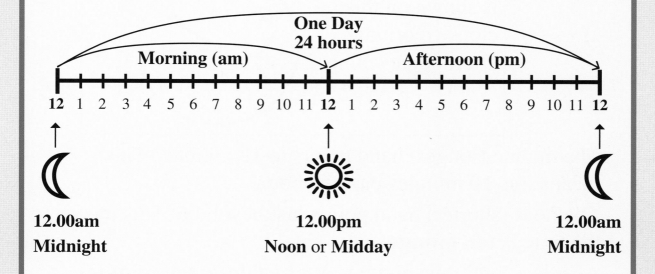

12.00am
Midnight

12.00pm
Noon or **Midday**

12.00am
Midnight

The analogue clock only shows **12** hours, so the clock will go round twice in a full day. This means all times are shown twice, but the only difference is 'am' or 'pm'.

First 12 Hours
Past **Midnight** up to **Noon**

Second 12 Hours
Past **Noon** up to **Midnight**

4.45am

4.45pm

b. Times of the Day

The day has a number of parts that each have a particular name.

The table lists these descriptions and times for the 12-hour clock.

Time of Day	12-hour Clock
Midnight	12.00am
Morning	12.01am-11.59am
Noon	12.00pm
Afternoon	12.01pm-5.59pm
Evening	6.00pm-11.59pm

Example: What time of day is shown on this clock (morning/ afternoon/evening)?

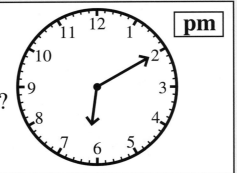

The minute (longer) hand points to **10** minutes. This means it is **10** minutes past the hour.

The hour (shorter) hand points just beyond **6**. This means the time is **ten minutes past six.**

As it is a 'pm' time and it is after **6.00pm, ten minutes past six** is an evening time.

Answer: **evening**

Exercise 15: 20

What time of day is shown on the clock (morning/ afternoon/evening)?

Score

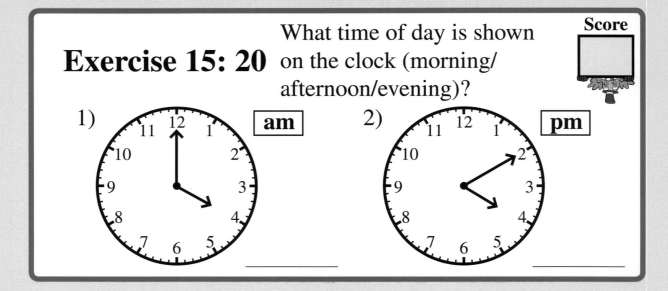

70

3) 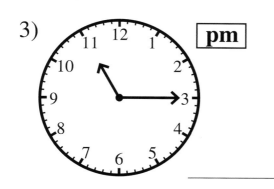 **pm**

_____

4) 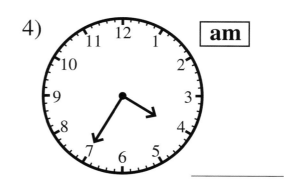 **am**

_____

5) 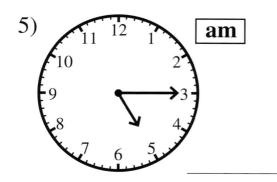 **am**

_____

6) 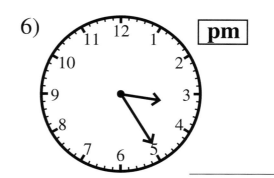 **pm**

_____

7) 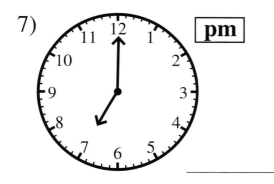 **pm**

_____

8) 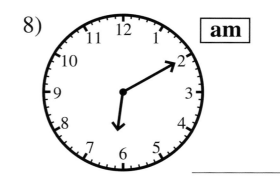 **am**

_____

9) 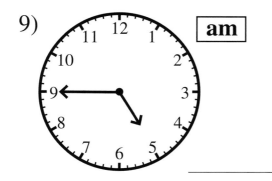 **am**

_____

10) 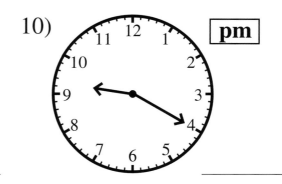 **pm**

_____

c. Writing Times in Full

Example: What time, in full, is shown on this clock?

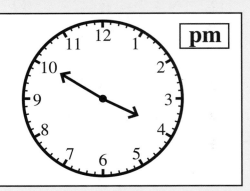

The minute (longer) hand points to **50** minutes. This means it is **10** minutes to the hour.

60mins – 50mins = 10mins

The hour (shorter) hand nearly reaches the number **4**. This means the time is **ten to four**.

It is a 'pm' time and is after **12.00pm** but before **6.00pm**, so it is an **afternoon** time.

Answer: **ten to four in the afternoon**

Exercise 15: 21 Write the time in full:

Score

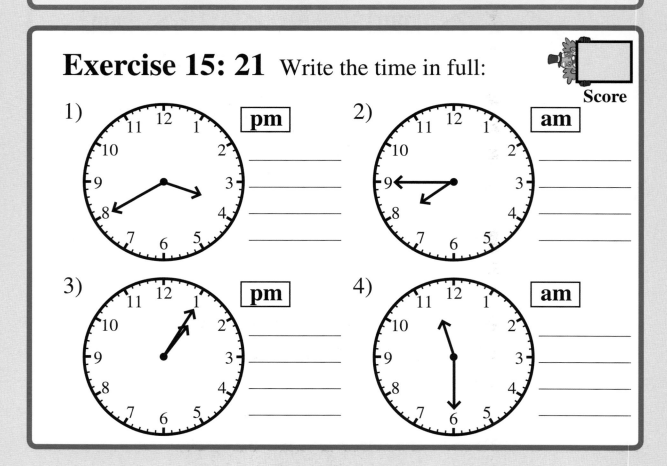

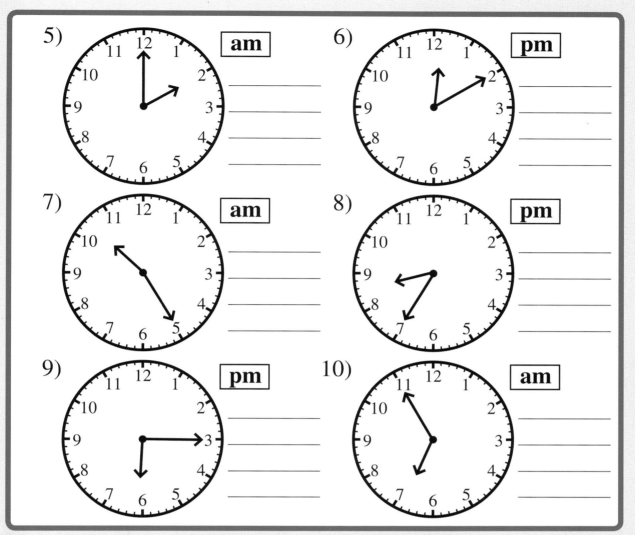

d. Writing Times in Figures

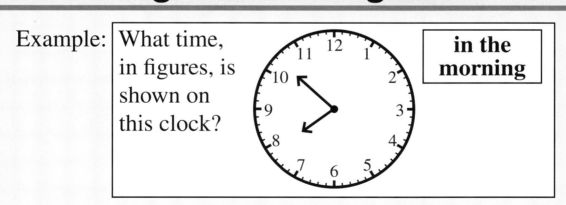

Example: What time, in figures, is shown on this clock?

in the morning

The minute (longer) hand points to **52** minutes.

The hour (shorter) hand has gone past the number **7** and nearly reaches the number **8**.

This means the time is **7.52**. It is in the morning, so it will be an 'am' time.

Answer: **7.52am**

Exercise 15: 22 Write the time in figures:

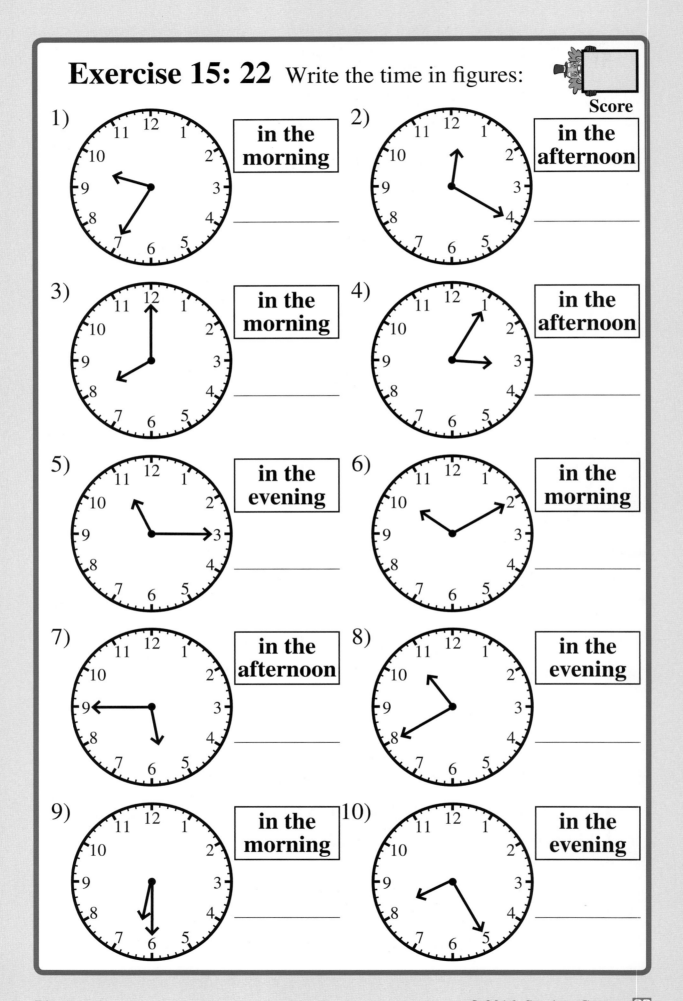

1) **in the morning**

_____

2) **in the afternoon**

_____

3) **in the morning**

_____

4) **in the afternoon**

_____

5) **in the evening**

_____

6) **in the morning**

_____

7) **in the afternoon**

_____

8) **in the evening**

_____

9) **in the morning**

_____

10) **in the evening**

_____

© 2016 Stephen Curran

5. 24-hour Time
a. The 24-hour System

The **24-hour System** treats the whole day as one complete period. This is shown on the diagram below:

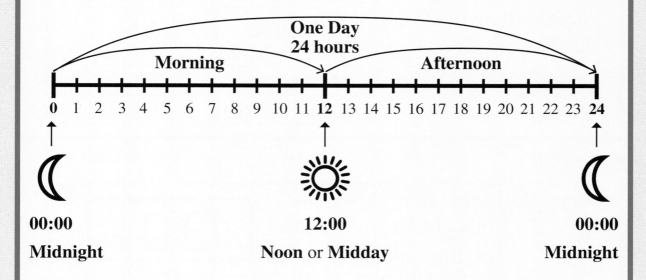

There is no need to use 'am' or 'pm' as each time only appears once in a day.

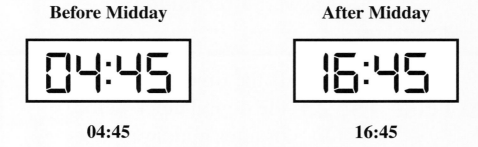

There are always four digits in a **24-hour** time. The hours and the minutes can be separated by a colon (**:**).

Most morning times have a **zero** at the beginning, except for **10:00**, **11:00** and **12:00**.

24-hour clocks or watches are often called digital clocks. This means the time is only shown using digits and there are no hands or pointers. Digital clocks are electronic.

b. Times of the Day

The 24-hour system is used on all timetables for buses, trains and aeroplanes. This makes it impossible to confuse whether the time is before or after midday.

The table lists the ways of describing time for the 24-hour clock.

Time of Day	Clock Time
Midnight	00:00
Before Midday	00:01-11:59
Noon	12:00
After Midday	12:01-23:59

Example: Is the time shown on this digital clock before or after midday?

Midday on a 24-hour clock is **12:00**. As the hour is greater than **12**, this means the time **13:01** is after midday.

Answer: **after midday**

Score

Exercise 15: 23 Is the time shown on the digital clock before or after midday?

1)

2)

3)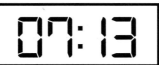

4)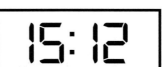

5) `05:36`

_____

6) `11:48`

_____

7) `20:21`

_____

8) `09:15`

_____

9) `22:46`

_____

10) `21:51`

_____

c. Writing 24-hour Times

The 24-hour clock runs from midnight to midnight. The inside clock shows the first 12 hours of a day and the outside clock shows the second 12 hours of the day.

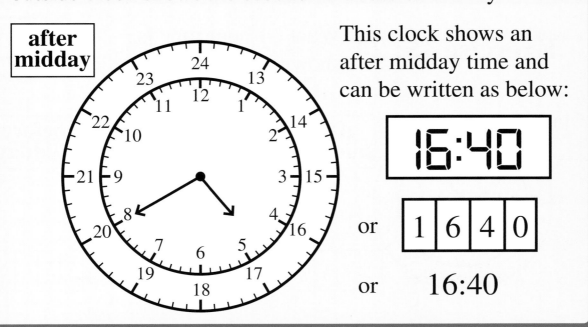

after midday

This clock shows an after midday time and can be written as below:

`16:40`

or | 1 | 6 | 4 | 0 |

or 16:40

Example: What 24-hour time is shown on this clock?

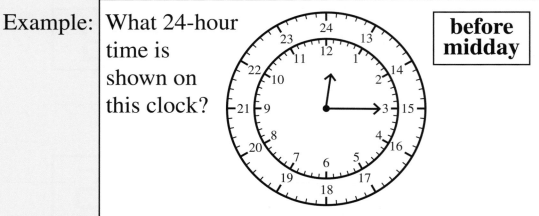

before midday

The minute (longer) hand points to **15** minutes. The hour (shorter) hand is just after the number **12** or **24**.

As this time is before midday, it means the time occurs just after midnight, which is shown on the clock face as **24** hours, but is always written as **00:00**.

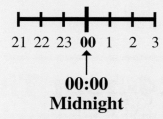

21 22 23 **00** 1 2 3

00:00
Midnight

This 24-hour time will be **00:15**.

Answer: **00:15**

Exercise 15: 24 What 24-hour time is shown on the clock?

Score

1)

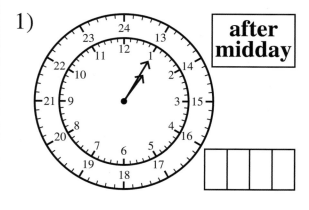

after midday

2)

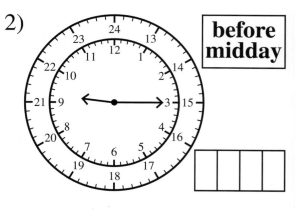

before midday

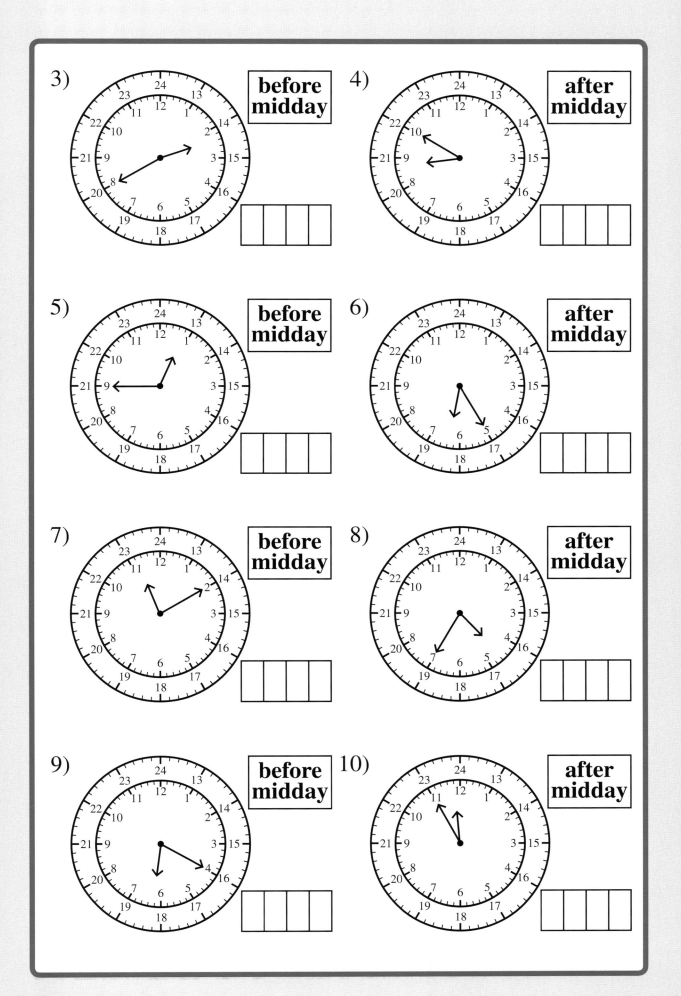

3) **before midday**

4) **after midday**

5) **before midday**

6) **after midday**

7) **before midday**

8) **after midday**

9) **before midday**

10) **after midday**

6. 12-hour & 24-hour Time
a. Conversions

It is important to be able to convert 12-hour time to 24-hour time and 24-hour time to 12-hour time.

The timeline below compares 12-hour with 24-hour time over a period of one day.

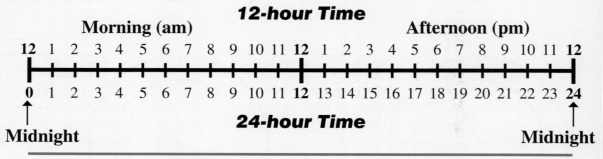

The table below shows some examples of 12-hour and 24-hour conversions:

12-hour Clock	24-hour Clock
12 midnight	00:00
4.30am	04:30
12.00 noon (midday)	12:00
2.15pm	14:15
11.59pm	23:59

(i) 12-hour to 24-hour Time

Example: Convert **6.37pm** to 24-hour time.

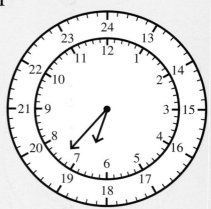

When converting 12-hour and 24-hour times, the minutes always stay the same. It will be **37** minutes.

As this is a 'pm' time, the hour time refers to the second **12** hours on the outer clock.

The hour hand points beyond **6** in 12-hour time, but in 24-hour time it points beyond the number **18**.

Answer: **18:37**

Exercise 15: 25

Convert the 12-hour time to 24-hour time:

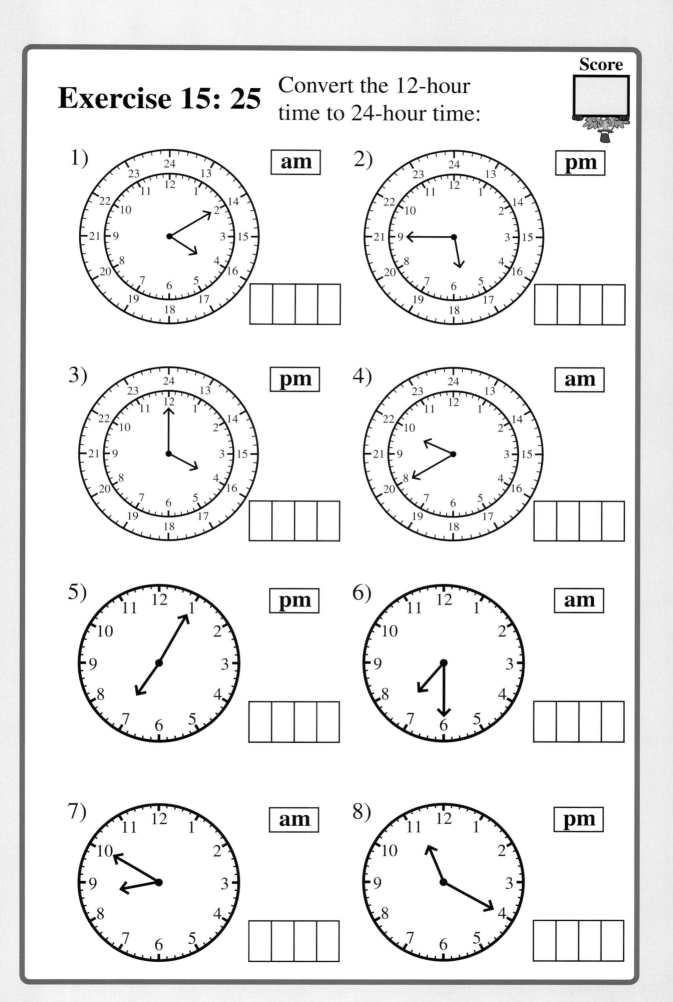

1) **am**

2) **pm**

3) **pm**

4) **am**

5) **pm**

6) **am**

7) **am**

8) **pm**

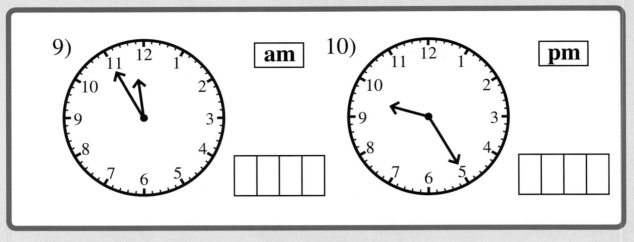

9) **am**

10) **pm**

(ii) 24-hour to 12-hour Time

Example: Convert **01:43** to 12-hour time.

When converting 24-hour and 12-hour times, the minutes always stay the same. It will be **43** minutes.

The hour **01** is in the first half of the day, meaning it is an 'am' time and the hour digit stays the same.

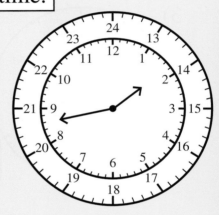

Answer: **1.43am**

Exercise 15: 26   Convert the 24-hour time to 12-hour time:

1) **22:15**

2) **05:50**

3) **02:28**

4) **18:43**

5) `12:09`

_____

6) `01:32`

_____

7) `13:17`

_____

8) `00:00`

_____

9) `06:52`

_____

10) `20:36`

_____

b. Time After

Example: What will the time be **30** minutes after this?

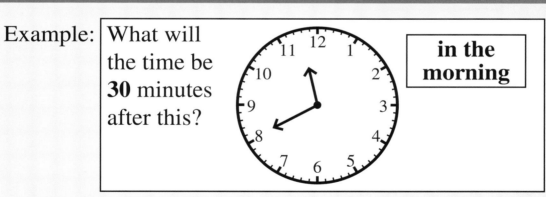

in the
morning

This clock shows the time **11.40am**.

The minute hand will move **30** minutes around the clock, from the **8** to the **2**, which is **10** minutes past the hour.

This time will be in the next hour, so it will be **12.10pm**. It has changed from an 'am' time to a 'pm' time.

Answer: **12.10pm**

Exercise 15: 27 Answer the following:

1) 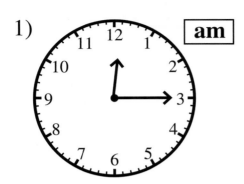 **am**

What will the time be
2 hours after this?

_____

2) 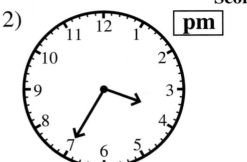 **pm**

What will the time be
30 minutes after this?

_____

3) **08:55**

What will the time be
1 hour after this?

_____

4) **09:00**

What will the time be
3 hours after this?

_____

5) 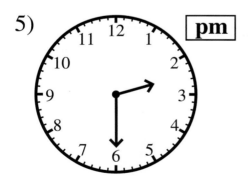 **pm**

What will the time be
$1\frac{1}{2}$ hours after this?

_____

6) 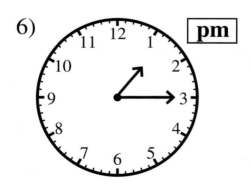 **pm**

What will the time be
$2\frac{1}{2}$ hours after this?

_____

7) `08:20`

What will the time be **4 hours** after this?

_____

8) `23:40`

What will the time be **5 hours** after this?

_____

9) 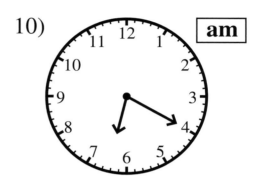 **pm**

What will the time be **3½ hours** after this?

_____

10) **am**

What will the time be **4½ hours** after this?

_____

c. Time Before

Example: What was the time **2 hours** and **30 minutes** before this?  `09:50`

This clock shows the time **09:50**.

Step 1 - Subtract the hours   **09 – 2 hours = 07**

Step 2 - Subtract the minutes   **50 – 30 minutes = 20**

Answer: **07:20**

Exercise 15: 28 Answer the following:

Score

1)  **pm**

What was the time
1 hour before this?

_____

2) 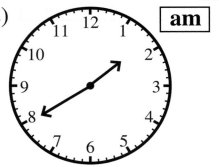 **am**

What was the time
4 hours before this?

_____

3)

What was the time
2 hours before this?

_____

4)

What was the time
$\frac{1}{2}$ hour before this?

_____

5) 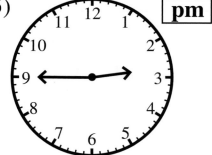 **pm**

What was the time
$1\frac{1}{2}$ hours before this?

_____

6)  **am**

What was the time
3 hours before this?

_____

7) **05:50**

What was the time
4½ hours before this?

_____

8) **14:30**

What was the time
2½ hours before this?

_____

9) 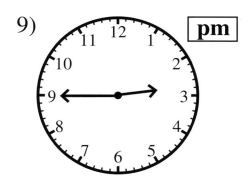 **pm**

What was the time
5 hours before this?

_____

10) 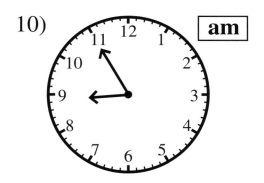 **am**

What was the time
3½ hours before this?

_____

7. Problem Solving

Example: | Marcia is catching a bus. The timetable shows the next bus is at **13:43**. What is this time in 12-hour clock?

The time **13:43** is an after midday time, meaning it will be 'pm'.

On the inside 12-hour clock the hour digits will change from **13** to **1**.

The minutes will stay the same.

Answer: **1.43pm**

Exercise 15: 29   Answer the following:

1) 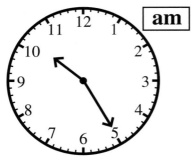 **am**

Alex looks at this clock. What time does it show?

_____

2)  **am**

What will the time be $2\frac{1}{2}$ hours after this?

_____

3) What is the time $1\frac{1}{2}$ hours after **ten to twelve** in the morning? _____

4) Naimah wants to catch a train at **8.15pm**. The timetable is written in 24-hour clock. How is this train time written on the timetable? _____

5) How many minutes are shown by the arrow?

_____

6) Fin's birthday is in August. It is currently April. How many months are there between now and his birthday? _____

7) On a note, the date **17/03/13** is written. How is this date written in full? _____

8) The cinema is advertising a showing of a film at **19:35**. What time is this film being shown in 12-hour clock? _____

9) On a board, the teacher wrote **10/06/16**. What is this date written in full? _____

10) Keith is catching a plane at **23:15**. What is this time in 12-hour clock? _____

Answers

Chapter Twelve
Percentages

Exercise 12: 1
1) 21%
2) 84%
3) 18%
4) 99%
5) Shade 62 squares
6) Shade 35 squares
7) Shade 77 squares
8) Shade 43 squares
9) 10%
10) 34%

Exercise 12: 2
1) 70% 2) 20%
3) 35% 4) 85%
5) 60% 6) 10%
7) 50% 8) 70%
9) 50% 10) 35%

Exercise 12: 3
1) $\frac{1}{2}$ 2) 20%
3) 30% 4) $\frac{2}{5}$
5) 10% 6) $\frac{7}{10}$
7) 25% 8) 90%
9) $\frac{3}{4}$
10) $\frac{8}{10}$ or $\frac{4}{5}$

Exercise 12: 4
1) 0.1 2) 50%
3) 30% 4) 0.75
5) 1 6) 25%
7) 0.4 8) 6%
9) 0.8 10) 1%

Exercise 12: 5
1) $\frac{1}{2}$
2) 20%
3) 0.25
4) 60%
5) $\frac{1}{10}$
6) 0.75
7) 30%, 0.3
8) $\frac{4}{5}$, 0.8
9) 70%, $\frac{7}{10}$
10) 90%, 0.9

Exercise 12: 6
1) 5p 2) 6
3) 20 4) 8g
5) 450 6) 100
7) £7 8) 5
9) 20 10) 50kg

Exercise 12: 7
1) 81
2) 360
3) 150
4) 63
5) 84
6) 4p
7) £165
8) 120kg
9) 320
10) 14g

Exercise 12: 8
1) £20
2) 4
3) 175mℓ
4) 80%
5) 12
6) 21
7) 10p
8) 350m
9) 84
10) 36

Chapter Thirteen
Probability

Exercise 13: 1
1) Impossible
2) Certain
3) Impossible
4) Possible
5) Certain
6) Certain
7) Unlikely
8) Unlikely
9) Likely
10) Impossible

Exercise 13: 2
1) Yes 2) No
3) Yes 4) Yes
5) No
6) Unfair
7) Unfair
8) Fair
9) Unfair
10) Fair

Exercise 13: 3
1) North, East, South, West
2) left, right
3) A, B, C, D
4) odd, even
5) red, blue, green, yellow
6) red, blue, green, yellow, white
7) 5p, 10p, 20, 50p
8) heads, tails
9) hearts, clubs, diamonds, spades
10) 1, 2, 3, 4, 5, 6

Exercise 13: 4
1) $\frac{1}{5}$ 2) $\frac{1}{5}$
3) $\frac{1}{6}$ 4) $\frac{1}{52}$
5) $\frac{1}{5}$ 6) $\frac{1}{13}$
7) $\frac{1}{2}$ 8) $\frac{1}{3}$
9) $\frac{2}{3}$ 10) $\frac{1}{2}$

Exercise 13: 5
1) $\frac{7}{10}$ 2) 6 tickets
3) $\frac{1}{2}$ 4) $\frac{3}{11}$
5) $\frac{1}{2}$ 6) $\frac{3}{10}$
7) $\frac{1}{6}$ 8) $\frac{2}{3}$
9) $\frac{4}{5}$ 10) $\frac{1}{7}$

Chapter Fourteen
Lines & Angles

Exercise 14: 1
1) diagonal
2) horizontal
3) vertical
4) c & g
5) a, d & h
6) 5
7) 6
8) 27
9) 4
10) 4

Exercise 14: 2
1) Parallel
2) Parallel
3) Perpendicular
4) Perpendicular
5) Perpendicular
6) Parallel
7) Perpendicular
8) Perpendicular
9) a, d, e, f, j
10) b, c, g, h, i

Exercise 14: 3
1) parallel
2) parallel
3) parallel
4) perpendicular
5) diagonal
6) perpendicular
7) vertical
8) vertical

Answers

9) parallel
10) horizontal

Exercise 14: 4

1)

2)

3)

4)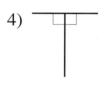

5)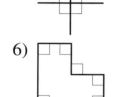

6)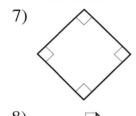

7)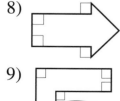

8)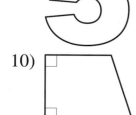

9)

10)

Exercise 14: 5
1) Yes   2) Yes
3) No   4) Yes
5) Yes   6) No
7) Yes   8) No
9) No   10) No

Exercise 14: 6
1) 4   2) 2
3) 1   4) 3
5) 8   6) 180°
7) 270°   8) 360°
9) 90°   10) 540°

Exercise 14: 7
1) wider
2) wider
3) wider
4) narrower
5) narrower
6) acute
7) reflex
8) obtuse
9) obtuse
10) acute

Exercise 14: 8a
1)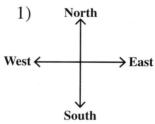
2) south-east
3) north-west
4) south-west
5) north-east

Exercise 14: 8b
6) west
7) north-west
8) north-east
9) north
10) south-east

Chapter Fifteen
Time

Exercise 15: 1
1) 730   2) No
3) 4   4) 156
5) 40   6) 366
7) 52   8) 21
9) 24   10) 28

Exercise 15: 2
1) March   3
2) January   1
3) September   9
4) May   5
5) December   12
6) August   8
7) February   2
8) October   10
9) June   6
10) April   4

Exercise 15: 3
1) January
2) February
3) March
4) April
5) June
6) August
7) September
8) October
9) November
10) December

Exercise 15: 4
1) July
2) August
3) February
4) May
5) March
6) January
7) November
8) 4

9) 3
10) 6

Exercise 15: 5
1) July   31
2) February   28
3) October   31
4) January   31
5) November   30
6) June   30
7) September   30
8) December   31
9) August   31
10) March   31

Exercise 15: 6
1) Saturday and Sunday
2) 2
3) Saturday
4) Tuesday
5) Sunday
6) Thursday
7) Wednesday
8) Friday
9) Sunday
10) Monday

Exercise 15: 7
1) 08.06.67
2) 22.09.96
3) 01.04.80
4) 14.02.15
5) 31.12.02
6) 28.07.73
7) 21.01.70
8) 04.08.87
9) 19.03.08
10) 03.05.13

Exercise 15: 8
1) 8th November 2015

Answers

2) 10th October 1996
3) 5th February 1962
4) 4th June 2011
5) 27th June 1997
6) 20th August 1962
7) 29th February 2016
8) 20th April 1954
9) 11th May 1994
10) 27th December 1965

Exercise 15: 9
1) Saturday
2) 7
3) Thursday 12th January
4) 5
5) Tuesday 24th January
6) 4
7) Friday 9th June
8) 7
9) Sunday
10) Tuesday 20th June

Exercise 15: 10
1) Sunday
2) Saturday 9th July 2016
3) Friday 9th September 2016
4) 5
5) Wednesday 16th March 2016
6) Thursday
7) Wednesday 14th September 2016

8) Tuesday 6th September 2016
9) Monday
10) Friday 4th March 2016

Exercise 15: 11
1) 120mins
2) 180mins
3) 270mins
4) 1hr 27mins
5) 1hr 43mins
6) 90secs
7) 240secs
8) 300secs
9) 1min 12secs
10) 2mins 23secs

Exercise 15: 12
1) 20 minutes
2) 25 minutes
3) 10 minutes
4) 35 minutes
5) 5 minutes
6) 30 minutes
7) 15 minutes
8) 45 minutes
9) 55 minutes
10) 40 minutes

Exercise 15: 13
1) Two o'clock; 2.00
2) Eight o'clock; 8.00
3) Five o'clock; 5.00
4) Six o'clock; 6.00
5) One o'clock; 1.00
6) Twelve o'clock; 12.00
7) Four o'clock

8) Seven o'clock

9) Nine o'clock

10) Eleven o'clock

Exercise 15: 14
1) Quarter past eight; 8.15
2) Quarter past two; 2.15
3) Quarter past five; 5.15
4) Quarter past twelve; 12.15
5) Quarter past four; 4.15
6) Quarter past three; 3.15
7) Quarter past nine

8) Quarter past six

Answers

9) Quarter past one

10) Quarter past eleven

Exercise 15: 15

1) Half past one; 1.30
2) Half past three; 3.30
3) Half past eight; 8.30
4) Half past eleven; 11.30
5) Half past seven; 7.30
6) Half past six; 6.30
7) Half past two

8) Half past five

9) Half past nine

10) Half past twelve

Exercise 15: 16

1) Quarter to three; 2.45
2) Quarter to eight; 7.45
3) Quarter to twelve; 11.45
4) Quarter to six; 5.45
5) Quarter to nine; 8.45
6) Quarter to five; 4.45
7) Quarter to four

8) Quarter to seven

9) Quarter to ten

10) Quarter to one

Answers

Exercise 15: 17
1) Ten past six; 6.10
2) Twenty-five past one; 1.25
3) Five past four; 4.05
4) Twenty past three; 3.20
5) Twelve minutes past eleven; 11.12
6) Twenty-eight minutes past eight; 8.28
7) Seventeen minutes past two; 2.17
8) Twenty-one minutes past twelve; 12.21
9) Two minutes past five; 5.02
10) Eight minutes past nine; 9.08

Exercise 15: 18
1) Five to two; 1.55
2) Twenty to six; 5.40
3) Ten to seven; 6.50
4) Twenty-five to nine; 8.35
5) Three minutes to one; 12.57
6) Fourteen minutes to twelve; 11.46
7) Twenty-one minutes to ten; 9.39
8) Twenty-nine minutes to three; 2.31
9) Eighteen minutes to eight; 7.42
10) Seven minutes to five; 4.53

Exercise 15: 19
1) two o'clock
2) quarter past nine
3) quarter to six
4) five to two
5) 11.20
6) 7.50
7) 12.25
8) half past six
9) twenty-five to twelve
10) 3.20

Exercise 15: 20
1) morning
2) afternoon
3) evening
4) morning
5) morning
6) afternoon
7) evening
8) morning
9) morning
10) evening

Exercise 15: 21
1) Twenty to four in the afternoon
2) Quarter to eight in the morning
3) Five past one on the afternoon
4) Half past eleven in the morning
5) Two o'clock in the morning
6) Ten past twelve in the afternoon
7) Twenty-five past ten in the morning
8) Twenty-five to nine in the evening
9) Quarter past six in the evening
10) Five to seven in the morning

Exercise 15: 22
1) 9.35am
2) 12.20pm
3) 8.00am
4) 3.05pm
5) 11.15pm
6) 10.10am
7) 5.45pm
8) 10.40pm
9) 6.30am
10) 8.25pm

Exercise 15: 23
1) Before midday
2) After midday
3) Before midday

Answers

4) After midday
5) Before midday
6) Before midday
7) After midday
8) Before midday
9) After midday
10) After midday

Exercise 15: 24
1) 13:05   2) 09:15
3) 02:40   4) 20:50
5) 00:45   6) 18:25
7) 11:10   8) 16:35
9) 06:20   10) 23:55

Exercise 15: 25
1) 04:10   2) 17:45
3) 16:00   4) 09:40
5) 19:05   6) 07:30
7) 08:50   8) 23:20
9) 11:55   10) 21:25

Exercise 15: 26
1) 10.15pm   2) 5.50am
3) 2.28am   4) 6.43pm
5) 12.09pm   6) 1.32am
7) 1.17pm   8) 12.00am
9) 6.52am   10) 8.36pm

Exercise 15: 27
1) 2.15am   2) 4.05pm
3) 09:55   4) 12:00
5) 4.00pm   6) 3.45pm
7) 12:20   8) 04:40
9) 9.45pm   10) 10.50am

Exercise 15: 28
1) 4.05pm   2) 9.40pm
3) 08:10   4) 12:05
5) 1.15pm   6) 5.05am
7) 01:20   8) 12:00
9) 9.45am   10) 5.25am

Exercise 15: 29
1) 10.25am
2) 1.40pm
3) 1.20pm
4) 20:15
5) 25 minutes
6) 4
7) 17th March 2013
8) 7.35pm
9) 10th June 2016
10) 11.15pm

PROGRESS CHARTS

Shade in your score for each exercise on the graph. Add up for your total score.

12. PERCENTAGES

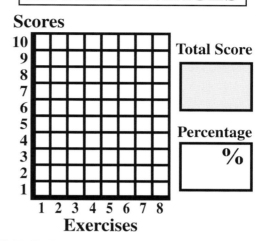

13. PROBABILITY

14. LINES & ANGLES

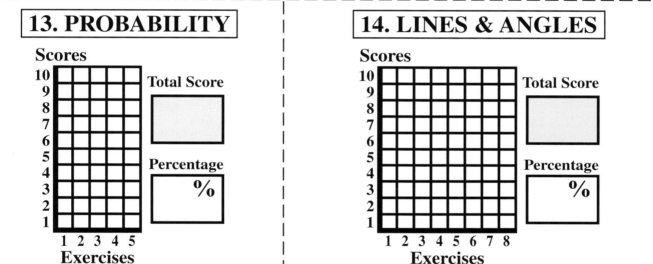

15. TIME

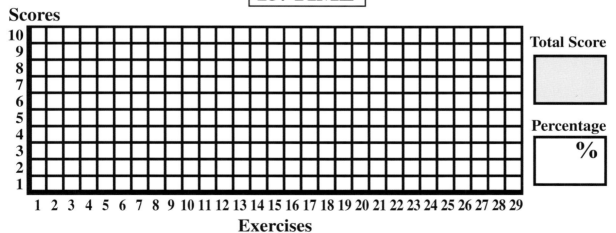

Overall Percentage %

CERTIFICATE OF

ACHIEVEMENT

This certifies

_____

has successfully completed

Key Stage 2 Maths
Year 3/4
WORKBOOK **7**

Overall percentage
score achieved

%

Comment _____

_____

Signed _____

(teacher/parent/guardian)

Date _____